Directing Amateur Theatre

Helen E. Sharman

A & C Black • London

First published 2004
A & C Black Publishers Limited
37 Soho Square, London W1D 3QZ
www.acblack.com

© 2004 Helen E. Sharman

ISBN 0-7136-6807-5

A CIP catalogue record for this book is available from the British Library.

A & C Black uses paper produced with elemental chlorine-free pulp, harvested from managed sustainable forests.

Typeset in 10/12pt ITC Officina Sans

Printed and bound in Great Britain by
Creative Print and Design (Wales), Ebbw Vale

Contents

Acknowledgements

Thanks go to my friends at Beaconsfield Theatre Group for their advice and support, and to Beaconsfield Fire Brigade, the Performing Rights Society and NODA for sharing their expertise.

Prologue

This book is written for those brave souls who, like me, spend their spare time in the seductive and dangerous world of amateur theatre. We seek the irreplaceable rush of adrenalin and euphoria that comes at the end of a successful performance, the camaraderie and pleasure that is to be found in a close-knit team, and, go on, admit it, we love the taste of fame. To achieve our goals, we expose ourselves to the risks of live theatre, with minimal guidance and no formal training.

There is no substitute for hands-on experience and you never stop learning, but the following chapters may help you to avoid some of the pitfalls that lie in wait for the unwary. Primarily designed for those who are coaxed, cajoled and arm-twisted into the role of the director, this guide through the maze of amateur theatre also offers comfort and reassurance to any thespian who voluntarily puts their head into the silken noose.

What is a director?

A director is to a play what a conductor is to an orchestra. Without a guiding hand, both end in complete disharmony. Nowhere is this more true than in the world of amateur theatre where the director is regularly expected to be all things to all members of the society.

Let's start by defining the words 'director' and 'producer' as they will be used in this book. More and more societies are turning to the terminology used by the professional theatre, and those are the definitions that will be used here.

The director is the artistic controller of a show. It is his/her job to create the 'feel' of the piece, from the way the actors deliver their lines, to the set design and the publicity image. It is the task of the producer, or production manager, to turn these images into practical and financial reality. The producer will organise the back stage crew, book the venue and ensure that all runs smoothly and within budget. For many amateur groups, however, the director is called upon to fill both roles and this book is written with them in mind.

Why do we do it?

By definition, members of an amateur theatre company do what they do for love rather than money. Amateur status has absolutely nothing to do with the standard of the final product. You may not receive financial reward, but the audience has paid to watch the show and deserves the very best that you can give. The worst comment that can be heard as the audience leaves is 'They were very good – for amateurs.'

Achieving a professional standard should be the goal of every dramatic society and this is no easy task. Amateurs have obstacles on the road to excellence in a way that professional actors do not. A professional can be single-minded about the theatre, this is their chosen career, whereas the majority of an amateur team have other things on their mind – like a day job. Rehearsals will be missed because of business appointments and it takes real energy to give a stunning performance when you have already done a full day's work.

Time is not on the side of the amateur. There is rarely the luxury of concentrated all-day rehearsals. Lines must be learnt in lunch breaks, on the train, or late at night. Props and costumes must be sourced on occasional free days. The set is often constructed in a ridiculously short space of time and technical rehearsal is rarely more that a few precious hours. Professional actors often have the advantage of previews. How often have you watched an amateur show begin to fly – on the last night – and wished that you had another four performances to go?

Amateur expertise is also limited. Talent aside, professionals have received vocational training. They have been drilled in the tools of their trade, from movement and voice production, to set design and lighting techniques. The amateur must learn through experience.

There is yet a further problem – money. All theatre is expensive. It can be argued that many professional shows are under-funded, but an amateur company will never have the resources to construct the perfect set, or hire the ideal costume. That said, poverty can be the mother of invention, releasing a flood of creativity that results in an effect far superior to the more costly alternative.

Amateur theatre is a dangerous pastime. Actors are sick in the wings, technicians scream in frustration, there are sleepless nights and by the end of the process the whole company is physically and emotionally drained. So why on earth do we do it?

The answer is that we love it! The feeling of triumph when some elusive piece of the puzzle falls into place, when the audience falls about laughing or gasps in fear, is unequalled. The sense of satisfaction and achievement as the final applause ripples through the auditorium is indescribable to someone who has never been there. The close knit bonds that grow between fellow sufferers lead to a level of trust and friendship that is rarely found elsewhere. To many part-time thespians, theatre is a drug – deprive us of our fix and we begin to wilt.

Are you ready to direct?

Everyone has to start somewhere, but before embarking on your first play, it is wise to take a long hard look at your skills and your experience. You should already have been on stage in a variety of shows. It is not necessary to have had a starring role, not all good directors can act, but you should have at least said a few lines and carried the odd spear, so that you understand what it feels like to be directed. It is advisable to have worked back stage and have a basic idea of what happens behind the scenes in terms of stage management, props, or costume. Ideally, you should have some knowledge of sound and lights. Even if you have never rigged a lamp, you should have some idea of what lights can do for a production. This may seem a tall order, but if you are to lead a team, you should know what each member can offer and where some of the key problems may lie. The last element in your self-imposed apprenticeship is to work as an assistant to an experienced director.

Finally, ask yourself how strong you feel. The role of director is often lonely and the weight of a show can result in stress and anxiety, especially when things are not going well. Advice will beset you from all sides and you will be called upon to make difficult decisions. You will have to think on your feet, sometimes with very little time to respond. When the curtain falls on the last performance, if the show has been successful, the cast will take the glory, but if it has not been up to scratch, you will be the one in the firing line. It really is 'tough at the top'.

After reading this, if you have not decided to take up a safer hobby, like parachuting or bungee jumping, and are still prepared to step into the abyss of amateur theatre, take heart. There is no greater feel of satisfaction and achievement than seeing the printed page come to life and hearing an audience applaud your efforts.

All the blood, sweat and tears will be worthwhile, so go for it!

ACT I

THE OPENING MOMENTS of a production set the tone for the whole performance. A strong beginning will engage the attention of the audience who will then settle comfortably in their seats for an enjoyable evening. Conversely, a hesitant start will make them uncomfortable and edgy – some will wonder why they bothered to come, some will turn their minds to other things and a few may actually doze off!

Your first act as a director is to decide on the play and on the team that will bring it to life. This apparently simple step, is actually the one that will have the most influence on the success of a production. Choose a play that does not inspire you, or a cast member who you are uncomfortable with, and you give yourself an up-hill struggle.

CHAPTER 1

Setting Out

THE FIRST CHALLENGE is to find a play, and, most importantly, find one that you like. The play needs to interest you and to excite your creative juices. An experienced director can turn their hand to most things, but until you are really sure of your craft, it helps to have a real passion for the piece. After all, it is going to occupy a good part of your waking hours (and some of the sleeping ones as well!) so you may as well enjoy it.

There are a lot of scripts out there, and it may seem like looking for a needle in a haystack. However, once you focus on what you like and what is possible for your company, the list will shrink to manageable proportions. Finding the right play takes time, but it will be time well spent.

A word of warning; there is no such thing as an easy play. True, some are more straightforward than others, but every script has its own challenge. The most difficult genre is farce, with comedies a close second. Some companies believe that a funny script will play itself – it won't.

If you have a play in mind, it is a good idea to arrange a play reading. A script can be promising in print, but lose its appeal when read aloud.

One-act or full-length?

This is usually dictated by your society's programme. A one-act play may have fewer pages, but will require as much commitment and planning as a full-blown production.

There are a fair number of one-act plays that will happily combine to make up an evening's entertainment. An occasional production of this type can provide the opportunity for new directors to test themselves out. Sharing the responsibility can make the experience less daunting, and if you are lucky, you could have the same amount of rehearsal time that is normally allocated to a full-length piece – luxury! Note the word 'occasional' – double bills do not seem to have the same attraction for audiences as a single play, so it is unlikely to be in your group's interests to do this on a regular basis.

Fitting the bill

The style of your chosen play may be dictated by your society's programme. Running plays of a similar genre back-to-back does not make for an interesting programme. Budget is also a key factor. Costume dramas and plays with complicated sets are expensive and most groups can only afford to do this type of play once every two or three years.

Be very aware of what plays are coming to your area, both amateur and professional. A mysterious thought-bubble can travel across your district, provoking an outbreak of Ayckbourn or Wilde, sometimes the identical play. Such duplication is bad for everybody's box office. National professional tours are also worth watching, since this may result in restrictions on the availability of performing rights.

The size of the stage and the time available for set construction should also be taken into account.

Potential cast

For most amateur groups, the size and age of the cast is often the deciding factor. The pool of members that you will have to draw on can fluctuate depending on the time of year. School holidays may automatically limit the availability of both cast and crew. An increasing number of amateurs belong to more than one society and the dates of other, overlapping productions can again restrict your choice. I recommend a few judicious phone calls to test the water before you make the final decision.

How to choose your play

There are two main sources of material – Samuel French and Josef Weinberger. Both offer comprehensive catalogues which include a brief synopsis of each play and most helpful, details of type of setting and cast numbers. Josef Weinberger also have a catalogue of musicals and a free loan service of perusal copies. Up to four copies may be available for a period of four weeks, but please note this is a popular service and titles are not always available.

Last but not least

You must *always* check that the performing rights are available before going any further. The publishing house will be able to tell you who to contact. Apart from the time that can be wasted by all concerned if you have begun rehearsal, only to find that you are unable to do the play, your group will have wasted money on scripts and probably, publicity.

Finally, order the scripts, arrange the auditions and start work.

CHAPTER 2

Auditions

AUDITIONS ARE PROBABLY the worst part of a director's job and also the most crucial. It is here that you set the tone for the whole production. This is true for any director, but more so for a first timer, so take the time to plan.

The members of your company want to see somebody who is not only totally conversant with the play, but who is calm and in control. This is no time to be flapping around with pieces of paper, hesitating and apologising every two minutes. Auditions should not only be a time for the would-be actors, but also a chance for those with an interest in back stage to put themselves forward.

Homework

Read the play again – and again. Make a list of the characters, their ages, appearance, and any key characteristics, so that these thumbnail sketches can be distributed in advance.

If possible, have copies of the script available before the event for anyone interested in auditioning. Select relevant passages for audition pieces and keep them short. Two pages of dialogue is about right. Your selection should take into account key speeches and cover the relationships of the characters. For example, if two people are supposed to be, or become, a couple, give yourself the opportunity of seeing them together.

Assuming that your auditions are done publicly, it is a good idea to take your 'audience' into consideration by having a variety of pieces. You may find it helpful to hear the same pages time after time, but they will fidget and talk less if you give them some variety.

Don't pre-cast. Every amateur director should have some idea of who might play what, but never give the impression that you have decided on your team before audition night. By all means, give likely candidates a call, but be careful to say that you would like to hear them read, and not 'I can really see you in that part'. If you then change your mind, the repercussions can be painful for both you and the disappointed actor. It is normally the task of the group committee to publicise the auditions and to book a venue, but there is no harm in double checking.

Audition panel

It is vital that auditions are seen to be fair and the panel is a key part of this process.

Three members, including the director, is a sensible number. Ideally, one should be a committee member and the third should be an established member of the group. All-male or all-female panels should be avoided, and relatives or spouses of auditionees should be automatically excluded.

The panel's task is to assist the director in selecting the best possible cast and to ensure that all the hopefuls are treated fairly. It is your job to ensure that your panel have an opportunity to read the script in advance and to talk them through the way you see the play and what you are looking for in a cast.

The Auditions

The panel should arrive at the venue at least 15 minutes early to allow time to arrange furniture, put papers in order and appear totally organised when the candidates arrive. Set a table and chairs for the panel away from the main entrance, but place the 'audience' seating near to it. A small point, maybe, but there will always be latecomers and it is sensible to allow them to slip in, rather than barge through in the middle of someone's big moment.

When the majority have arrived, call the room to order and, if necessary, introduce yourself and your panel. It may sound obvious, but do repeat the dates of the show and rehearsal nights. You should then check round the room and make a note of holiday dates, and other commitments. Make sure that you have contact numbers for everyone present, particularly newcomers.

Next, give a brief synopsis of the play and the way you see it. This is an ideal opportunity to comment on the back-stage elements, whether props are straightforward or challenging, period costume or modern dress, interesting set/lighting design and so on. It is no use having a brilliant cast if there is no crew to support them. Follow this with an outline of the characters.

Now comes the moment of truth. Take each character in turn and make a list of who wishes to audition. Appoint one of the panel to take notes of who reads and to keep track of the passages that they are given. Your candidates should come forward as required and be encouraged to act out the scene. If the scene calls for it, provide a chair or similar prop to help this process. As director, it is your right to direct – even at auditions! There is nothing in the rule book that says you cannot ask someone to repeat the speech, slower, faster, or even in a foreign accent. Not everyone is good at sight reading, and not everyone can take direction. You will have to work with this cast, so you may as well discover if they can work with you.

Take a break, ideally for coffee and biscuits, when you have seen all the candidates at least once. This will give the panel time to take stock, decide if there are any combinations/pairings that it would be useful to see, and to check that everyone has read their fair share. The word 'fair' cannot be repeated often enough. Any audition, particularly in the world of amateur theatre, is emotionally charged. Someone will always be disappointed and it is far easier to handle rejected colleagues if you have been seen to be completely even-handed.

When you have heard as much as you feel appropriate, ensure that you have not inadvertently missed someone by asking if anyone wishes to read more. This strategy will also put a stop to any disappointed candidate complaining that they did not read as much as someone else. Now turn your attention to the back-stage team. Hopefully, many who auditioned will also be happy to turn their hand to another aspect of the show. Make it clear that volunteering for such a job does not mean that they will not be considered for a part.

Before everyone, except the panel, vanishes to the nearest pub, tell them when you expect to announce the details of cast and crew.

Decisions, decisions

It may be that the audition panel can retire to a separate room and cast the play there and then, but never feel pressurised into making snap decisions. If at all possible, at least give yourself time to sleep on the casting before going public. Aim for the best possible cast, but bear in mind that perfect casts are very rare. Sometimes the team falls easily into place, but when you are forced to choose, the following factors may help.

1. Availability v ability:

self explanatory, but sometimes it is better to choose a really good actor who is away for a fortnight during rehearsals, than someone who is going to struggle with the part.

2. Experience v enthusiasm:

again, it is worth giving serious consideration to a newcomer who has shown themselves willing to learn, rather than a seasoned member who may not be so flexible.

3. Team player v Prima Donna:

amateurs act for pleasure. You may have a brilliant actor who has a reputation for upsetting their fellow thespians. Cast them by all means, but do it with your eyes wide open.

4. Buggin's turn:

if all else is equal, then someone who has just had a major part should probably be rejected in favour of a member who has worked hard for the group without the reward of a recent stage appearance.

Breaking the news

Call everyone who auditioned on the day you said you would. It is good practice to make all the calls yourself and to contact everyone on the same evening. It is easy to call with the offer of a part – calls to the unsuccessful are more difficult and you may find yourself leaving them till last. Personally, I find it helpful to alternate the congratulations with the disappointments.

You cannot please all of the people all of the time and there are times when a group member or two will be unhappy with the panel's decision. Nobody said the theatre was fair.

When things go wrong

The most common problem at this stage is that you are one cast member short. Don't panic! Resist the temptation to announce the team that you have, unless you are 100% sure that you will not need to shuffle them from one part to another. There is nothing worse than offering a part and then taking it away again.

Time is not on your side and you should aim to complete your cast within a week, or at most two. Any longer and you lose too much rehearsal time. The only exception is if the role is very small. Your odds on finding someone to learn half a dozen lines and not fall over the furniture are good and you can afford to wait.

Run through your membership list first of all. It may be that the ideal candidate was unable to attend the audition, was unaware that it was happening, or simply did not see themselves in the part. Step two, is to look outside the group. Talk to your panel, to other members, contact other local societies and generally use the power of the am-dram grapevine that exists in many areas of the country.

Auditions

In the happy event that you find a potential candidate, it is good practice for them to undergo some form of audition. It is obviously not sensible to take someone 'sight unseen' and even if you are familiar with their work, you need to put them through their paces. Again, this is part of being seen to be fair. The best solution is to reassemble your panel and run a second audition. If this is not possible, have at least one other member present, and do your very best not to take the decision on your own. In the event that a cast member is forced to drop out during rehearsals, invite the potential replacement to a rehearsal and share the decision with the cast.

If you are unable to cast to your satisfaction, it may be best for all concerned to abandon the play. This may sound drastic, but sometimes there is no alternative. As a director, you must consider not only your reputation, but the reputation of the group. For example, if you are short, as often happens, of a male juvenile lead and all you have is an actor of 50 – don't do it!

ACT II

THEATRE IS ALL about communication, not only between cast and audience, but in every aspect of the production. Good communication is essential for a team to work efficiently and has the added benefit of creating a happy atmosphere – after all, we do this for pleasure! Misunderstandings and confusion lead, at best, to less than satisfactory results; at worst, to a back stage atmosphere that you can cut with a knife.

It is up to you, the director, to lead by example, to give clear instructions and to be decisive, but also to be aware of any problems that your vision may create and to be prepared to compromise. Most amateur directors are well aware of the acting side of things, but often have a limited experience of technical issues. An awareness of the language and jargon used by the crew, and a basic grasp of their roles, can only improve your working relationship and significantly benefit the end result.

The following chapters will not turn you into a lighting designer, or a publicity expert, but they offer some insight into the myriad tasks that go to create a production. They may also trigger some new ideas that will lift a production from the ordinary to the special.

CHAPTER 3

The Assistant Director

THE ROLE OF assistant director in amateur theatre varies considerably, not simply from group to group, but between different directors. Sometimes there is an assistant and a prompt, sometimes one person fills both roles. An assistant can have major input into the direction of the piece, taking rehearsals on the director's behalf, or simply sit on the sidelines of rehearsals to take notes and record moves. Many groups find this position a means of training potential new directors, while some are so low in personnel that the job does not exist. Flying solo is far from ideal, no matter how experienced a director you are and, unless your company is really thin on the ground, the benefit of a second pair of eyes at rehearsals is enormous.

The working relationship

However you choose to work, it is essential to clarify your expectations from the outset. A good relationship between director and assistant is a key ingredient for a successful production and clear communication is vital. Aim to meet with your assistant before the first rehearsal and come to a mutual decision as to how this particular partnership is going to work and perhaps establish a few ground rules. You can then share your ideas about the play, the set, characterisation and so on. And keep talking! Arrive a few minutes early for rehearsals and stay on after the cast has gone home to share your thinking about what needs to be done, or your reactions to the evening's work. This constant dialogue helps to ensure that you are both working towards the same goal and minimises conflict.

Even with a very experienced assistant, it is important to keep the line of authority clear, otherwise you may confuse your cast. The two of you should agree that any suggestions that the assistant makes should be made quietly to you, not directly to the actors, and any disagreement over the direction, however small, will be dealt with outside rehearsal. Be prepared to listen to new and different ideas, indeed, your assistant should be encouraged to express an opinion, but you must both be very clear that the final decisions rest with you, the director.

Recording moves

The assistant should use a dissected script, interleaved with plain paper to record the moves and any other additional comments. This may seem like a duplication of the work that you have already done, but there are inevitably going to be changes and it is much easier to work out a complicated section of blocking if you are not trying to write it down at the same time.

Unlike the professional theatre, amateurs tend to devise their own system of short-hand for recording moves. This is fine, provided that it is intelligible to someone else, should your assistant be unable to attend a rehearsal.

At the risk of teaching my grandmother to suck eggs, it is worth defining the jargon that is used to describe the areas of the stage – stage right, up stage and so on. Many first-timers will have no idea what you are talking about and some seasoned performers can get confused. Stage Right and Stage Left are taken from the actor's point of view as he faces the audience – so Stage Right is to the director's left as he watches the rehearsal. It may sound complicated, but you do get used to it, although I confess, when working as an assistant and filling in for an absent cast member, I have often had to turn my diagram of moves upside-down to make sense of it! Up stage is towards the back of the stage, Down stage is nearest the front. The reason for these terms goes back to the time when many stages were raked, sloping down from the back towards the auditorium, so the actor really did move either up or down.

The following system, using the terms mentioned above, seems to work for many groups:

The abbreviations of US for up stage, DSR for down stage right, are easily understood, X–R, for cross to stage right is also straightforward but not all moves are as easy to annotate, particularly when there are several members of cast involved. In that case, try drawing a skeletal set plan at the top of the plain page, indicating the furniture and the exits, and use character initials to mark the relative positions of the cast. This 'map' can then be read at a glance and saves precious rehearsal time. As the characters move, indicate the direction, mark the new position and give it a number. The same number is then written against the relevant line of the text. Be careful not to record so many moves on the same map that you end up with something that looks like an algebraic equation! For a busy piece of action, it will be necessary to draw a series of maps indicating the relative positions of the actors at varying points in the text. Always work in pencil, and have an efficient rubber – directors change their minds!

Once basic blocking is complete, a good assistant frees you to concentrate on the finer detail without constantly having to refer to the script. As hand props make their appearance, your assistant can keep track of where glasses have been left, where a handbag was placed, or where an ashtray has to be. He should make a note of any additional items that are not on the original props list, and generally act as your back-up memory. Directors have a great deal to remember and rarely remember everything.

Words, words and more words

Once the actors start to get to grips with the lines and books go down, the assistant becomes indispensable. It is not possible to develop a performance if the actor is clutching a book, and the presence of a prompt allows them to begin this process and to stagger through the half-learnt script without holding up rehearsals,

Prompting requires fierce concentration. An actor who is desperately struggling for a line will not appreciate a prompt who has lost her place, neither will they be happy if she continually interrupts to correct every slight paraphrase. The middle section of rehearsals benefit from being allowed to flow as much as possible, on the other hand, give your prompter clear permission to stop the cast if they have jumped ahead, or delivered a speech that would be unrecognisable to the author. Mistakes that escape at this stage can become embedded and hard to unlearn.

The classic actor's nightmare is to find yourself on a stage without the faintest idea of what play you are supposed to be doing, let alone what words are supposed to come out of your mouth. This dread of going completely blank lies at the very heart of stage fright. Anyone, professional or amateur, can 'dry' and the heart-stopping seconds that follow are agonising for both actor and audience. You and your prompter cannot prevent this happening, but there are some things that you can do to minimise the risk.

Building trust

The aim of a prompt is to make herself redundant. She serves as a safety net for the cast, and like a net, should only be used in emergencies. For his part, the actor, like a high-wire artist, needs to have complete confidence that she will catch him if he falters. Use rehearsals to create a bond of trust and understanding, for it is often true, that the stronger the relationship between cast and prompt, the less likely they are to need her.

As rehearsals progress, scenes will begin to run at a good pace, despite paraphrasing and lines that are omitted. At this stage, a prompter who jumps in at every opportunity can destroy confidence, so ask her not to interrupt the action, but to make a note of the glitches and point them out at the end of the section. There will be occasions where an actor knows what he is supposed to say, but struggles for the precise wording. There are times when it is best to remain silent and let them dig the words from their memories, there are others when they really, really need a hint. Rather than assuming that the prompt is completely telepathic, each actor should arrive at a form of signal – some call 'Line' or 'Prompt', others will simply make eye contact. These signals should slowly become redundant as a good prompt learns how each actor behaves under stress – the body language, the hesitation in the voice, the glazed look about the eyes. By show week, she will have developed a sixth sense as to when she should intervene.

She should make a note of trouble spots. A wiggly line beside the speech can be rubbed out once the problem is resolved, any of these lines that remain at the time of performance are a useful reminder to be extra-vigilant.

At one of the final runs, probably the week before the performance, warn the cast that they will be working without a prompt and swear her to silence for the evening. This gives everyone a flavour of how you expect them to behave on the night – obviously, if the actors lose it completely, the prompt will step in, but you don't need to tell them that!

On the night

Discuss the best position for your prompter with the stage manager. She should not get in the way of cast and crew entrances and she should be able to see at least some of the action. Prompting blind is a possible, but a nerve-racking experience. Prompting, as we said before, requires intense concentration, and the stage manager should ensure that there are no distractions, no whispered conversations behind her, and certainly, no one should talk to her while the play is in progress.

If the worst happens and an actor needs a prompt, then it should be given in as few words as possible, sometimes one word is enough, and most important of all, it should be loud. The actor will be experiencing intense anxiety, and a whispered line is unlikely to get through the fear. A prompt that has to be repeated will have the audience squirming in their seats with embarrassment and will do nothing for the actors' nerves. A prompt is a prompt and whilst it cannot be hidden from the audience, if it is clear, and picked up fast, it will be forgiven and forgotten.

The decision to prompt must be taken in the space of two or three seconds. Nobody likes taking a prompt, and your assistant can find herself in a no-win situation – speak and be told later by a furious actor that he did not need it – stay silent and be shouted at for leaving him stranded. All she can do is her best, and if she makes a mistake, she may need you, the director, to soothe and support her.

CHAPTER 4

The Production Manager

THE TITLE OF production manager is rarely used in amateur companies. Instead, the complex and all-embracing task of overseeing the smooth running of a production usually falls to the director, or even the group chairman. It is a job that must be done by somebody and I strongly recommend that this individual is not the director – you have enough to worry about!

The ideal candidate for this position is a person who has been a member of the company for at least two years, preferably longer, and who knows the members and the local area well. They will have worked back stage in some capacity, sat on the group's committee, perhaps acted, and it is a bonus if they have directing experience.

They should be organised, patient, diplomatic and be good at problem solving.

The job

The best production managers appear to actually 'do' very little. The title 'manager' says it all. They are there to ensure that everyone else on the team does what they are supposed to, that deadlines are met, and budgets adhered to. The production manager works in partnership with the director, but with different responsibilities. In general terms, the director deals with the artistic elements of the show, while the manager is in charge of the business aspect. There are a number of grey areas which can be covered by either, but it remains the manager's job to ensure that things happen.

This is the hardest job to describe – the best I can come up with is the theatrical equivalent of 'How long is a piece of string?' The relatively short length of this section in no way reflects the extent of this role. In a perfect world, everyone will do exactly what they are supposed to, and she will have a smooth ride. However, experience suggests that this rarely, if ever, happens. The production manager can be called upon to fill in for any department, to deal with practical problems, and, at times, will need to pour oil onto the troubled waters of personal conflicts. In summary, expect the unexpected!

The production manager can be chosen ahead of the auditions, but it is more usual for someone to volunteer for the post when casting is completed. The golden rule of production management is – 'Check everything that moves.'

First things first

1. Check that the venue has been booked for the correct dates and times.
2. Check that rehearsal rooms have been booked, again for the correct dates.
3. Check the arrangements for entering the rehearsal rooms – organise a key for the director if necessary.
4. Check that the performing rights for the play are available and that the royalties have been paid.
5. Check that the correct number of scripts are available and arrange for additional copies to be ordered for back stage if necessary.

Early rehearsals

1. Produce a list of names and contact numbers of all cast and crew involved in the show. Given that the group will have a membership list, this piece of paper may seem like overkill, but it is a handy reference document that makes life easier for all concerned. The contacts should include mobile numbers and e-mail addresses where applicable. Not everyone is happy to be contacted at work, so always ask the person concerned before publicising an office number.

2. The manager can also take responsibility for collecting any monies due to the group – subscriptions, rehearsal fees, money for the script.

3. Check that a rehearsal schedule has been circulated. This task will usually be done by the director, but in the event of a large cast and a busy director, and the inevitable changes to the schedule, it is wise to check that everyone is aware of when they are needed.

4. Arrange for coffee! Most groups take a break during the evening, and in rehearsal venues where coffee is not available, it should be the manager's responsibility to ensure that some form of refreshment is on hand. This is not as simple as it sounds, for depending on your cast, you may be asked for decaffeinated tea and coffee, specific sweeteners, even soya milk!

The manager does not have to appear at every rehearsal and can appoint a deputy for this task. However, arriving at coffee time provides a useful opportunity to talk to the director, to gauge the atmosphere of the cast and to pick up any possible problems. For this reason, it is worth making the effort to attend at least one rehearsal a week.

Back stage meetings

The manager should call at least two back stage meetings. The first should be held as soon a possible, the second can be called about ten days before show week. Whilst the heads of departments and the director will have talked to each other, there is no substitute for getting everyone in the same room.

The first meeting should include:

> Director
> Set designer
> Stage manager
> Property manager
> Wardrobe manager
> Sound
> Lights
> Publicity
> Treasurer

The assistant director is not essential to this process, but should be involved if at all possible. The other key individual, the front of house manager, is unlikely to be needed until a later meeting.

The meeting needs a chairman who can be either the manager, or the director and it should have an agenda.

The main goals of this meeting are:

1. To set affordable and realistic budgets for each department – hence the presence of the treasurer.
2. To set deadlines for relevant departments.
3. To anticipate problem areas.

In between meetings, the production manager needs to have her finger on the pulse of the production and in consequence, may find herself living on the phone! It is helpful to set up a check-list to help keep abreast of deadlines and dates for the collection of items, and also the dates by which they have to be returned. She should have a working knowledge of all the various departments, at least in terms of their brief for this particular production and should be the first point of contact if things go wrong. Sorry, this is amateur theatre – the last sentence should read '*when* things go wrong'! She should keep you fully informed of progress, or lack of progress and, in return, you should continually feed relevant information back. Good communication is paramount, but this is easier said than done. Never, ever make assumptions and always, always check.

The second meeting

The assembled company will be the same as before, with the addition of the front of house manager.

The aim of this meeting is to treble-check that each department is moving according to plan, to identify any remaining problems, and to solve them. Now is the time to check that any transport required has been booked and that there is a willing volunteer to drive. The personnel for the set build, and the front of house team should have been organised in advance of this meeting, but there is still time to fill in any gaps.

Set-up and show week

The production manager should be in attendance for the greater part of the set-build, if not all of it. This is the time when small problems can be blown out of all proportion, and she should be prepared to mediate, fetch, carry, make tea, in fact anything that will keep the build running smoothly!

Our company has a policy of providing sandwiches and drinks for the technicians at the set build and the technical rehearsal. This falls to the production manager to organise, as does arranging for bottles of water (and cups) to be in the dressing room for the actors during the run.

The production manager can also serve as the liaison officer with the venue. Any problems should be passed to her to deal with, either from the venue manager to the company, or vice versa. This is far more efficient, and effective, than random members of the team carrying messages which will probably get lost, or go to the wrong person.

During the show the production manager needs to do very little, unless of course, she has an additional job. She should have already discussed the process of strike (taking down the set) with the stage manager, checked that transport is available if needed, that a crew has been organised to dismantle the set, and who is responsible for the return of hired and borrowed items.

Strike

The production manager should put in an appearance to ensure that all items are being returned to their rightful owners, and that the venue has been left in good order. Then, and only then, can she relax!

CHAPTER 5

Publicity Matters

THEATRE NEEDS AN audience. There is no point in working for weeks on end to produce a show that only a handful of people come to see. The audience will not arrive by magic; they must be given accurate advance information, interested in what is on offer, persuaded to buy a ticket, and last but not least, motivated to turn up on the night. This task usually falls to the group's publicity manager, but as a director, you need to be happy with the image that is presented to the public and may well have input into the wording of the handbills and the programme.

The image

The play has been decided, the dates, times and venue confirmed. The first task on the agenda is to select an image for the publicity material. You may have a very clear idea in your mind, but do not get too dogmatic, for the final choice is not yours to make. The publicity manager is responsible for the corporate identity of the group and a whole season of plays, your mind is focussed on only one. However, time permitting, you should have an opportunity to check a proof.

Posters and handbills have to work fast. They have only a few seconds to attract attention and encourage further reading. The ideal design will be un-cluttered, interesting to look at and easy to read. Handbills, in particular, convey, not only an impression of the play, but the overall image of the society. They are the first tangible indication of the professionalism of the group. A flimsy, badly designed handbill screams village hall am dram at its worst and although you may be amateur and may indeed perform in a local hall, this is not the image that you want. Go for the best quality paper your group can afford and take trouble with the design and accuracy of the information.

Colour can add instant impact to a poster, but colour printing is expensive, so if you really must jazz up your poster, confine yourself to coloured paper. Day-glo colours may well make your poster stand out, but can be totally inappropriate to the show you are promoting. While well suited to panto-mime, farce and comedy, luminous orange is not the right background for serious drama. Sepia tones, brown print on cream paper suit productions set in a by-gone era, such as *Cider With Rosie* by Laurie Lee, or Old Time Music Hall.

Typeface is also very important. Use too many styles of lettering and the image becomes cluttered and confusing, too few, and it is harder to isolate the key information. As a general rule, priority of size and density should go to the title of the play, the venue, dates and the box office number. The name of the group is important, but should not dominate the poster – it is not the main selling point. Check the licence agreement carefully, since the type size of the author's name is often specified, and you may find you have to include a 'by arrangement with' clause as well.

Handbills and posters should carry identical images, and be similar in colour. However, handbills have two sides and can carry additional inform-ation about the play. If the piece is not well known, give the potential audience a flavour of its style and content – whether it is a farce, a tear-jerker, warm, funny, and so on. The synopsis from the catalogue will often provide a useful starting point. Above all, keep it short, make it interesting and don't give away too much of the plot! Whether you are invited to write the blurb or not, again, you should have a chance to see the draft version before it goes to print.

Some groups use the reverse of a handbill to include a booking form. This seems to work best if you are lucky enough to have a large catchment area. The format should be a simple grid of dates and prices, and do remember to include the box office address and who the cheque should be made out to. The only way to find out if booking forms are a useful tool for your group is simply to try the idea for a season and monitor the response.

Size matters

Posters normally come in two sizes – A3 and A4. It is worth ordering a combination of both, since shops often have limited window space and prefer the smaller format, whilst key sites like libraries and town notice boards need A3 for the poster to have maximum impact.

Handbills are traditionally A5, but there is an increasing move to create them in 'DL' size, or $\frac{1}{3}$ of A4 (i.e. 99mm x 210mm). This format is elegant, and has the advantage of slipping into the plastic holders that are used in places which regularly display promotional material.

Design sources

1. Printing companies
Companies such as Cowdalls of Crewe carry an extensive list of existing images for specific shows.

2. Original art work

You may have an artistic individual, even a graphic designer within the group who will come up with the goods.

3. Original photographs

With the arrival of digital cameras and computer technology, it is now possible to take and adapt your own pictures. In a recent production of *When We Are Married* by J. B. Priestley, we found an Edwardian wedding group and superimposed the faces of our cast.

4. Images from the Web

It may seem tempting to download and use an image that you have found in an on-line gallery, but beware, the vast majority of these are copyright and should not be used without following proper procedure.

Distribution

Posters and handbills should be available at least a month before the production. They are absolutely no use to anyone in their box, so make sure they get distributed. First and foremost, make sure that your cast and crew are well supplied. It is far easier to sell a show when you are directly involved and with very few exceptions, the bigger the cast, the bigger the audience. Publicity officers are familiar with the display sites in their home town, but do not always attempt to increase the coverage to outlying places and this is definitely worth doing. If someone is interested in a production, they are willing to travel a few miles to see it.

Potential sites:

Shops
Libraries
Pubs and restaurants
Offices, banks, estate agents, some garages
Schools, colleges, evening class centres
Waiting rooms – doctor, dentist, train and bus
Public notice boards

Other ways of making handbills work for you include mailing lists, door to door leafleting, and publicity mornings.

The press

Local papers are a vital element in the publicity process. The most important piece of advice that I can give here is to talk to the papers well in advance and find out about deadlines. The best story or photograph in the world will end in the waste paper bin rather than the front page if it arrives too late. Many papers have deadlines well ahead of publication date, particularly the arts pages which are planned and written sometimes as much as two weeks in advance.

Even if you have a made all the deadlines, there are no guarantees that your story will appear in print. The only thing that can be done is to make your story interesting and whenever possible, arrange a photo call to accompany it. As the director, you should be consulted about the angle you wish to take with the press, indeed, you may even be asked to write it.

Finding an angle

Human interest is a popular approach. Perhaps one of your cast has had to lose weight, increase weight for the part, shave off a much-prized beard, or have their hair drastically cut or coloured? You can then offer a picture of the 'victim', perhaps before and after. At least the suffering actor will have a few days of glory for their pains. Perhaps they have had to undergo special training for the role – learn to tap dance, stage fight work, you get the idea.

Always, always make sure that the individual is happy for their picture to appear, and if the actor is female, never give their address or phone number, particularly if they are to appear provocatively, or scantily clothed. It is sad, but true, that a female can receive nuisance phone calls, or worse, as a result of careless publicity.

Unusual props or costumes can form the basis for a story. We have asked for a Russian *samovar*, a spinning wheel and a pair of size 13 slippers, among others. Sometimes you really do need the item, but more often you simply need the press coverage. Advertising for items in this way does occasionally produce the goods, but don't rely on it.

Children and animals always go down well. *The Wiz*, the musical version of *The Wizard of Oz*, calls for a small dog to play Toto. We ran a 'doggy audition' and the press featured a dozen hopeful dogs and their owners. Again, although we advertised for canine candidates, there was little interest, so dog owners known to the group were invited along to ensure that we did indeed have a picture. Luckily, the initial request was seen by a professional trainer and her small shaggy friend. We secured the services of a highly-trained dog and achieved a second picture of the 'successful applicant' a couple of weeks later. For *On Golden Pond*, we had a delightful picture of the grandfather and the young boy on a fishing trip. Actually, it was staged at a local pond that held nothing more than a few tadpoles, but it looked good.

That brings us to the subject of location. It is far better to find an appropriate and interesting location for your press call, than to use a boring rehearsal room as a back-drop. For example, for *The Play's the Thing* by Molnar, set in the 1920s, one actor was required to be a butler. We persuaded a local restaurant with perfect art deco décor, to allow us to snap our actor, apparently being taught the art of silver service by their head waiter. Never be afraid to ask, people are surprisingly cooperative, and after all, they get publicity too.

Running a press call

The details should be organised by the publicity manager, but you will probably want to go along to oversee the proceedings. You should be given details of the arrangements in time for you to liaise with wardrobe. Even if the precise costume is not available, always try to find an acceptable substitute – amateur actors in everyday clothes are not usually interesting, and rarely glamorous.

Be there on time, preferably about 15 minutes beforehand. Press photographers have tight schedules and if you and the relevant cast are late, they may leave for the next job without your picture. Discuss the pose in advance with the publicity manager and the actor(s). The photographer will appreciate your efficiency.

Do not overcrowd the picture. One actor can be quite sufficient, but more than four will result in a confusing image. Who you select for the picture will depend on their character and availability, but you cannot, and should not, invite everyone. Explain to your cast why you have selected some individuals, but not others, apologise to anyone who feels rejected and be firm.

Always have a handbill with the show details available for the photographer. While the picture is being taken, someone should make a note of the names of the subjects and where they are standing. Give this and the handbill to the photographer at the end of the shoot. This again to saves time, looks professional, and hopefully means that the names are correctly spelled!

You may have more than one paper in your area. If so, think of a different pose and story for each of them. Papers are competitive and you risk having your shot rejected if the editor knows that his rival is going to run the same thing a couple of days earlier.

If, for some reason, it is not possible to arrange a mutually convenient time with the press, it is worth asking if the paper will accept one that you have taken. Check what size they prefer, black and white or colour, when it should arrive at the office and to whom it should be sent. If the publication are happy with an e-mail version, check what format their computers use.

The press release

Find out the name of the relevant reporter or arts editor, do not send your precious details to nobody in particular and trust to luck. The chances are that nobody will read it.

Always:

1. Type the release, post it, or use e-mail, then call the paper a day or so later to ensure that it arrived.
2. Keep it short and to the point. Busy reporters do not have time to wade through a flowery essay to extract the key details.
3. Double check the dates, time and venue of the performance.
4. Include box office details and ticket prices.

If you have an interesting angle, use it. Be careful not to exaggerate, and avoid words like 'brilliant', 'unbelievable', 'outstanding' – your audience may not agree with you.

Presentation

A mailed press release should look professional and be easy to read. As with poster design, avoid blinding the reporter with a range of fonts, italics and capitals. Sending your release on letter-headed paper can give an air of professionalism, coloured paper may catch the attention, wide margins and double-spacing make it easier to read.

If you send copy by e-mail, avoid using coloured backgrounds or multi-coloured lettering. It does nothing except make it harder to download, and often extremely difficult to read.

Programmes

Programmes, like smartly dressed Front of House staff, set the tone of the evening. A well printed, interesting programme signals to the audience that they are about to watch a group who take their work seriously. A glossy 8 or 12 page programme may seem expensive, but you can charge a little bit extra, and with the help of advertising revenue may even make a profit. Interestingly, glossy paper not only looks good, but greatly improves the final print quality, especially in the reproduction of photographs.

The director's task is to write some form of introduction for the programme. It is usually up to you whether this is light-hearted, or takes a more serious tone, but you must establish with the publicity team how much space is available. This is your opportunity to put the audience in a receptive mood for the play they are about to see. You can include for example, a history of the play, why it is important to you, a few interesting facts about the author, or perhaps something that happened in rehearsal, but never, never apologise.

The following example may give you some ideas :

> '*The Cocktail Party* has fascinated me for more years than I intend to admit. It has more layers than an onion and at every rehearsal we have found something new. Edward says 'This is not what I expected' and for me, that sentence encapsulates the essence of the play.
>
> T. S. Eliot leads his characters from the deceptive safety of drawing room comedy and sends them on a journey of self-exploration, a journey sprinkled with love, humour and tragedy. The heady mix of the banal and the esoteric, reality and illusion, presents an enormous challenge for director and cast alike. I have been privileged to work with a dedicated cast who have been frequently seen pacing up and down and talking to themselves, as they came to grips with Eliot's delicious blank verse. The crew have finally escaped from beneath yards of muslin and have enabled us to add a few unexpected touches of our own. As for what it all means – that you must decide for yourselves.'

Audiences enjoy knowing something about the cast and, space permitting, a 'Who's Who', complete with photographs is a welcome addition to a programme. You can choose to print a simple informative biography, but when the production lends itself, you can have fun with the style of this information. For a production of *Laying the Ghost* by Simon Williams, the director suggested that each biog included words like 'haunted' and 'spirited', while a production of Adrian Mole could have each piece written in the style of a school report.

It is sensible for the director to check a proof of the programme, not only for spelling mistakes, but to make sure that all the relevant people are included. Your production manager, if you have one, should also check the details. Apart from crew members, it is important to acknowledge all those who have helped towards the production, from local businesses, to someone who has donated a prop, or given invaluable advice.

Reviews

Local papers regularly print reviews of amateur shows, but never assume that a critic will automatically arrive. If they are not invited – they won't come. It is unsafe to assume that your press release is enough to alert the relevant person, since local reviewers are often freelance and not working side-by-side with the arts editor. Your publicity manager should contact the paper and send a specific invitation. A reviewer will expect a complimentary ticket or two, and should be given a programme on arrival. It is not possible to write an accurate review without the names of the cast.

Critics make actors nervous, so don't tell the cast that there will be one in the audience until the performance is over. On the night, by all means introduce yourself, but do not hover, and certainly, never sit with him or her. Don't be tempted to seek them out at the end of the performance looking for compliments or, worse, to make excuses. If the review is unfavourable, resist the urge to ring the paper and berate the editor, it will only serve to make you and your society look thoroughly unprofessional, and may even affect your chances of reviews in the future.

CHAPTER 6

Set Design

IT IS IMPOSSIBLE to begin rehearsals of a play without having a clear idea of the set that you will be working on. As a director, you need to know where the exits and entrances are likely to be, where the windows are, if any, and whether there are stairs, or raised areas – all these elements must be decided before you can begin to think about blocking.

A set should meet two main requirements:
1. It should serve the needs of the play.
2. It should be practical for both cast and crew.

The process of set design

Set design is the result of collaboration between director and designer. In the amateur field, the designer often fulfils the role of stage manager and can also be in charge of the set build. If this is not the case, then the other people, or person, must be included in the discussions. Your role is to give the designer a clear idea of the feel of the play and how, ideally, you would like it to look. I say 'ideally' because one of the designer's tasks is to tell you what you can and cannot have.

First, you come up with your concept of how you want your production to look and then share your ideas with the designer. He will then take the proposal away and establish the feasibility of turning your vision into reality. You should then be presented with a set plan, complete with measurements. Once this has been agreed in principle, your final task is to bring in the lighting designer to ensure that he has no technical issues with the placement of flats and such like. Then, and only then, do you have the set plan that will form the basis for your blocking.

Creative design

The vast majority of scripts available to amateur companies include a set plan at the back. It is not essential that you follow these to the letter, indeed, the proposed design may not be feasible at your venue, so be open to considering something different.

Your first consideration is the area in which you intend to perform. You have a number of options:

Directing Amateur Theatre

1. The traditional stage with the audience in front of the action.

2. Place the action in the centre of the auditorium, surrounded on all four sides by the audience.

3. Perform, using one of the auditorium walls as a back-drop, with the audience on three sides.

4. To use both the stage and floor area with the audience on three sides.

5. To use the stage, but with the audience on stage surrounding the action.

6. Finally, for the adventurous, there is the possibility of a promenade performance where both actors and audience move from scene to scene.

For most groups, the venue will dictate this decision, but consider whether the apparent restriction is essential or if it is simply because your company have always done it this way. A little lateral thought and you may surprise yourself. A word of warning, don't be different for the sake of it – make sure that the performance area matches the play and be very sure in your own mind that you have the skills to direct successfully in a different format.

Let me give you a few examples where an unusual choice of acting area complemented the production. *Agnes of God* by John Pielmeier can work extremely well as a studio production with the audience on three sides. The intense emotions are heightened by the proximity of the actors to the audience. A local operatic society were brave enough to break with tradition and performed *Orpheus in the Underworld* using the stage to represent the earth and to seat the orchestra, while the bulk of the action in the underworld was played on the floor, with the audience on three sides.

The most usual construction for interiors is the box set – three walls constructed from individual flats that represent a room. Whilst this design is effective, it is not always essential. For a production of *The Killing of Sister George* by Frank Marcus, we designed a set that did not have a flat in sight. Instead, the walls were created by black drapes with strategically placed pictures hung on fishing wire, to create the impression of solidity. The illusion of a room was completed by suspending a chandelier above the stage.

For Eliot's *The Cocktail Party*, discussed in more detail in the section on lighting, the walls were muslin drapes and in the first act there were no visible doors or windows. This design was intended to give the impression of a closed environment with no apparent way out. However, in the last act, when much of the uncertainty of the opening has been resolved, we dropped

Set design

in a window, complete with drapes, and introduced doorways to suggest that the characters now had an opportunity to move on.

Even when the script appears to call for a living room, you can sometimes put your own stamp on the production by ignoring the obvious. For example, we mounted a production of *When We Are Married* by J. B. Priestley, not in a living room, but in the conservatory of the house, and *The Importance of Being Earnest* by Oscar Wilde can be taken into the garden. If it is possible to introduce a variety of levels, then do so. Levels will offer the opportunity of creating more interesting stage pictures. The variation in height can give the impression that actors on different levels are isolated from each other, and can also be used to indicate the relationship of characters – normally, the actor in the highest position will be seen as dominant, but this is another of those rules that can be broken!

Plays that need the set to represent more than one location in rapid succession present different challenges to a designer and the director alike. Shakespeare is the classic example, and the stage adaptations of Terry Pratchett's *Discworld* books by Stephen Briggs fall into the same category. Remember, you are in the business of illusion, so don't worry too much about flats and backdrops – set changes every few minutes, however fast, slow the action and disrupt the flow of a play. Simply create the feel of a throne room or a blasted heath by using lights, music and one or two well-chosen props.

The main set should be kept simple, but a variety of levels with steps and ramps to help the actors move easily from one area to another will add interest. These levels can become an integral part of the scene. In a production of *Daisy Pulls It Off* by Denise Deegan, we used a basic set which had a four-foot high walkway across the back of the stage, with a flight of stairs on either side. The main stage area was used for scenes within the school, the top level was used for the picture gallery and gave the Headmistress a wonderful dominant position for her assembly address. It also served as the cliff top, and the girls 'climbed' and battled their way up the stairs, which were now clearly a steep and slippery bank.

If you have the luxury of a mid-way curtain, and/or an apron stage that is in front of the main curtains, then your opportunities expand. It is now possible to make more major scene changes behind a curtain, whilst the action continues in front. These changes must be fast and silent. You should discuss these aspects with the stage manager, and make sure that the crew have time to practice the manoeuvres, preferably before technical rehearsal. Some of the tools of the trade for swift changes are:

1. Trucks: basically a rostrum on wheels that can carry a pre-set scene such as a desk and chair for an office, a throne or a banqueting table.

2. Revolve: this does exactly what it says. The circle of wood on wheels can be divided into two, or even three sections, each bearing the props for a different scene.

3. Flying: if you have access to the area above the stage, and beams or scaffolding of sufficient strength, then painted back cloths can be dropped in, as can curtains, flags, and so on.

Practical design

The best set design in the world is of no use at all if it is impractical for your venue.

The set plan in the book may have an entrance marked as stage left, but, if you have a brick wall on that side of the stage, you will have to rethink! If, as we do, you have good wing space on one side of the stage and not the other, then shift the entrances accordingly. If you slavishly follow the book, you may discover that you have half a dozen actors playing sardines before coming on stage, and that the trays of food and glasses that must be brought on are endangered by the lack of space.

Wing space, or more often, lack of, is easily forgotten by directors and the more complex the set the more important the issue becomes. Think before you ask for a particularly large piece of set, or furniture. Do you actually have space to store it without completely blocking the wings?

A stage carpet may deaden the sound of clumping boots, but it can also make complex set changes a nightmare. If you have a one-set play set in an interior, use it, but for a multi-set piece go back to bare boards. A stage floor should ideally be painted matt black – a gloss finish will reflect the lights. It may be possible to change the look of the floor by using painted hardboard to suggest tiles, or Astroturf to suggest grass.

If the cast are required to move in and out of doors at high speed, your designer and stage manager need to know so that they can plan for additional bracing. It is very embarrassing if apparently solid walls wobble every time someone slams a door!

While on the subject of doors, handles are much easier for nervous actors with sweaty palms to manage than knobs. The theatrical convention is that doors open onto the stage. This is not always possible, but which ever way it opens, make sure that this is established during the rehearsal period, as well as which side the handle will be – actors can lose all power of thought and have been known to pull when they should push!

Water, water, everywhere!

Some plays, notably *Steel Magnolias*, cannot be staged without running water. The mechanics are not that complicated, garden pond pumps and reservoir tanks back stage will fit the bill. However, these contraptions take up valuable wing space and demand extra safety precautions – water near lights and cables is a bad idea. The play which probably demands the most water is *Neville's Island* by Tim Firth. We first established that the stage was structurally strong enough to carry the weight of water, and then with the aid of a heavy duty pond liner, created a 'stream' down one side of the stage and across the front of the stage. The illusion of water could have been created by Perspex sheets, but would not have been so effective. However, a hapless aerobics class who used the auditorium during the run of the show thought that it was indeed Perspex and a number of ladies went away with soaking handbags!

Final touches

It is a fact that, at some level, audiences are aware of anomalies, even if they cannot put them into words. Attention to detail is imperative if you want a really good set. The view from a window is a classic example. Unless you are fortunate to have a really good scene painter, keep the view as simple as possible – trellis with greenery, a tree branch, even a lamppost are enough to suggest the outdoors. In the tension of the moment, even seasoned actors have been known to put their hands through what is supposed to be solid glass, so if you have windows, do try and make the effort to 'glaze' them with plastic sheet, Perspex or even gauze.

The last stage of constructing a set is to dress it with pictures, rugs, throws, umbrella stands and the like. It is worth recruiting someone with a good eye as your set dresser, this could be the stage manager, the property mistress, or someone completely different, even a member of the cast. Appropriate pictures, pot plants and ornaments can make a world of difference to a set, turning it from a sterile structure into a credible location. For *Laying the Ghost* by Simon Williams which is set in a retirement home, we added 'Fire Exit' signs, a sign indicating the location of the bar, and a busy notice board.

Once the set has been dressed, you should check that there no obstacles for your cast by walking the stage yourself. Look out for stray magazine racks and waste paper bins that can trip the unwary. Rugs bring a set to life, but make sure that they are taped to the floor and will not turn into a hazard. Plants look wonderful, but the heat of the lights can wreak havoc, so check that someone has been appointed to water them after each performance.

The detail is not only important to the audience, it is equally important to the cast. Our *Laying the Ghost* notice board was only visible to a third of the audience, but the cast felt it helped them to believe in their imaginary surroundings. Headed note paper on a writing desk and correctly addressed envelopes will be completely invisible to the audience, but will be appreciated by the actors.

The blood, sweat and tears that goes into constructing a really good set is made worthwhile when the audience bursts into spontaneous applause as the lights go up.

CHAPTER 7

The Stage Manager and Playing Safe

IGNORE THE STAGE manager at your peril! This post is absolutely essential to the smooth-running of any production. The cast can be at their peak, but if the curtain does not rise on time, props are misplaced and the gunshot explodes in the wrong act, then they may as well not have bothered. This is not a job for a raw beginner. A stage manager should have a good working knowledge of all aspects of back stage work. That way, he will better appreciate the problems of other departments and is more likely to have the respect of cast and crew.

The precise job description of this key role seems to vary considerably among amateur groups. In some societies the stage manager is often in charge of both set design and construction, in others, he may also be required to record moves and prompt the actors, as well as being responsible for assembling the crew and running back stage meetings. The position can be used as a catch-all for any job that does not have a name attached to it and as a result, stage managers may be hard to find.

Whatever the job description in your group, you can make show week run a great deal smoother if you have some understanding of quite how much this hard-pressed technician has on his plate.

Responsibilities

1. Safety:

It is his responsibility to ensure the safety of the cast and crew.

2. Set construction:

Whether the stage manager has designed the set or not, he should be involved in the build. He cannot easily take responsibility for problems during the run if he does not understand how the set was put together.

3. Technical rehearsal:

He should have control of this rehearsal and make sure that any problems are resolved. Ideally, he will have seen at least one full run of the play, so that he can plan in advance and make best use of the time. If this has not been possible, he must work very closely with the director.

4. Time keeping:

He must keep a close eye on the time and keep cast and crew informed prior to curtain up. He must also check that all personnel are at the theatre at least half a hour before the start of the performance.

5. Coordination:

He should be in contact with lights and sound to ensure that cues are accurate. He must also check that actors are ready in the wings for their entrances.

6. Strike:

He should oversee the dismantling of the set.

Safety first

It is the stage manager's task to minimise any risk to cast or crew throughout the production process. Venues will have their own lists of do's and don'ts and your SM should make himself familiar with any specific conditions. Some groups can be cavalier about their attitude to safety, but remember, break a fire regulation or a rule of the venue and the fire officer, or the theatre manager, would be within their rights to close you down.

The following is a list of the more common hazards but is not intended to be exhaustive. More detailed advice on safety precautions in the theatre is available from the Health and Safety Executive, contact details are listed at the back of the book.

1. Fire

Scenery should be flame proofed. Whilst modern flats are constructed from treated materials, it is advisable to use fire proof paint. Drapes and up-holstery should be sprayed with flame retardant. Greenery or dried foliage should also be sprayed.

Smoking is only allowed on stage when it is an integral part of the action. That means no wandering about with a hammer in one hand and a cigarette in the other. When there is smoking on stage, each ashtray should contain wet sand and there should be someone standing in the wings with a fire extinguisher. If you must use candles with a naked flame, check the regulations and follow them to the letter.

The stage manager should be familiar with all the fire exits from the stage and the procedure for evacuation of the venue. Where there is a safety curtain – use it!

2. Lighting

The technical crew should check the safety of the lights as they rig, but there is no harm in double checking that each lantern has a safety chain and that there is no damage to plugs and cables. Cables should be taped to the floor so that actors, and depending on the location of your sound and lights, audience, cannot trip and injure themselves.

The back stage area should have sufficient light to work in, but not so much that it spills over into the acting area. Sometimes it is helpful to use a small desk light to illuminate the props table or the quick change area. These lights should either have blue bulbs, or be masked with blue gel, and pointed away from the stage. Blue bulbs have less glare. They illuminate the area but have less 'spill' than normal bulbs. If your theatre has stairs that are poorly lit during performance, tape the edges with white or silver to make the steps easier to see and avoid accidents.

3. Pyrotechnics

Explosions on stage are fraught with danger. The pyros used in pantomime for the appearance of the genie should be treated with serious respect and only handled by someone who really knows what they are doing. The pods should be clearly marked out so that actors do not, literally 'put their foot in it'. They should not be placed anywhere near an exit point, or close to any item of scenery or drape that could catch light. The person appointed to trigger the effect should have a clear view of the stage and should only fire when everyone is in a safe position. In the event of the device misfiring, it should be disconnected and left for at least 15 minutes.

4. Smoke machines

Smoke can be produced by machines that use either dry ice, solid carbon dioxide, or fluid. Dry ice should be handled with insulated gloves since it can cause severe burns. As with everything else, the machine should not block exit routes, and neither should the smoke it exudes. Try and direct the smoke away from the auditorium to avoid choking your audience!

5. Scenery

All scenery should be securely braced so that there is no likelihood of a flat tumbling onto the cast. This sounds screamingly obvious, but I have seen a 12 foot flat topple slowly, and inexorably, onto the stage during a performance. No one was hurt – but they could have been. Likewise, if part of the set is supposed to collapse, the SM should take sensible precautions. One of the most effective 'collapse' effects that I have ever seen was in a production of *The Rape of the Belt* by Benn W. Levy. Theseus is locked in a tower, and must break out through the impenetrable stone wall. The tower looked as if made from a solid flat, but when the moment came, Theseus burst out scattering huge bricks left right and centre – they were created from cleverly painted shoe boxes! If your set requires that the stage area be extended, the stage manager must check and double check that no fire exits will be obstructed.

6. Small props

Props that are breakable should be stored carefully, well away from errant actors. If glass is broken on stage, deliberately, or otherwise, it must be cleared away at the first possible opportunity. Hot liquid should also be treated with caution and avoided if at all possible.

7. Guns

Replica guns, whether they can fire blanks or not, should be treated with the same respect as if they were real. One of the crew should be appointed to take charge of the weapon, hand it to the actor for the relevant scene and take it back immediately afterwards. While not in use, the weapon should be securely locked away.

8. Furniture

Any furniture or pieces of scenery should be stacked to allow clear access to the stage. Even with subdued light backstage, actors have a tendency to become blinkered and lose all coordination! Nothing must be allowed to obstruct a fire exit.

9. People

Unless their presence is required in the next page or so, actors and crew should be firmly discouraged from cluttering up the wings, sitting on the furniture, fiddling with the props and above all, from talking. From the technical rehearsal and throughout show week, the stage manager has control, and as you can see from the preceding list, he has a great deal to do. You and your cast can best help by keeping well out of the way. When scenery or furniture is on the move, the stage crew have priority. When the SM is struggling to deal with some problem from the lighting gallery, he does not need to be distracted by cast gossiping in a corner.

Set up

The stage manager should be heavily involved in the building of the set, even if he is not either the designer, or in charge of the construction team. As discussed earlier, he must minimise potential safety hazards, but perhaps more importantly, he can minimise emotional explosions by keeping the atmosphere positive and stepping in when the almost inevitable conflicts begin to brew. A set under construction is not a sensible, or safe place for people who have lost their temper!

The title is stage *manager*, yet it is often the managing element that disappears at this time. An ideal SM will endeavour to keep everybody busy, get things done in a smooth sequence and keep an eye on the time. A tall order, but if people have given up their time to do little other than pass the odd hammer, they can become disgruntled. If things are done in the wrong order then jobs may have to be done twice. Forget the time and you end up with a mad scramble.

As the director, you should be there to make suggestions and offer opinions, but remember, you are not in charge of the stage. By all means, make it clear what you want, but ultimately, it is the stage manager who will tell you what you can have.

When the set is complete, props can begin setting out the furniture. Once it is arranged to everyone's satisfaction, the stage manager, or props, should mark the position of each item. Things can, and do, get moved, either because of a set change, or because someone needs to adjust a drape, or paint a skirting board. Items that are out of place can throw an actor, so everything must go back to its appointed place. Accurate positioning is also important for lights, particularly if a special light has been trained on a chair. Electrical tape will do the job, either on boards or on carpet, and where there is more than one setting, use a different colour for each scene to avoid confusion. Keep the tape marks small and unobtrusive.

Technical rehearsal

The running of a technical rehearsal will be discussed in detail in a separate chapter, but it bears repeating that from the moment he arrives at the theatre, the stage manager, *not* the director, is in charge. Help him to do his job by planning in advance.

A key job for the stage manager is to check the sight lines so that the audience are not treated to a sneak preview of an actor pacing in the wings. Actually sit, don't stand, in a variety of seats at the edges of the auditorium to work these out. The SM can then put a line of masking tape on the floor to indicate the danger zone.

The stage manager should remind his crew that they should be dressed in black, with no potentially luminous white stripes in evidence, and that soft-soled shoes are preferable to heavy boots.

On the night

It is advisable for the stage manager to run a register of cast and crew. This can be a formal signing-in book, or a list of names pasted up in the dressing room. It is all too easy to lose track of people in the countdown to a performance and realise that someone vital is missing with only 20 minutes to go. The list also has obvious benefit in the event of a fire.

He should be one of the first to arrive, ideally an hour before. He should check that the stage floor is clean and that the props are all where they should be. Many venues have a community use by day and some unthinking users may have moved furniture, or left lost property and rubbish on your pristine stage. It happens. He needs to check with his team that all is in order, from props through to sound and lights. Half an hour before curtain up, he should give cast and crew the half hour call. At this point, everyone should be there. He should give a 15 minute call followed by a 10 minute call, and finally call for beginners on stage, five minutes before the start.

At this point, he needs to liase with the front of house manager that the audience is seated. A final check with his team, and the curtain can rise.

Few plays allow the stage manager to relax during performance. He must check that actors are ready and waiting for their next entrance, about two pages beforehand. Never rely on a tannoy system to the dressing room, nervous actors can go deaf as well as blind! Always call them in good time, it is not uncommon for a page or so of dialogue to go missing. He should also keep his eyes open for obstacles that mysteriously appear, and for last minute problems.

Finally, the ideal stage manager must be organised, patient and a serious diplomat. He must have full authority, something which you as director can reinforce. He should have the ability to remain calm in a crisis – a stage manager who panics can send waves of fear and uncertainty throughout the team.

CHAPTER 8

Dressing the Part

THE CLOTHES THAT we wear in everyday life express our personalities and the same is true of actors. First impressions are particularly important in the theatre and costume offers the audience a short-cut to the heart of the character, allowing them to make instant judgements about social class and personality. Clothes give clear messages about time - the historical era, the season of the year and the passage of time. The style and colour of the costume can be used symbolically to enhance the atmosphere of a piece and to emphasise relationships between characters.

The wardrobe manager

Whenever possible, always have someone in charge of the wardrobe and do not be tempted to go it alone. Even if your play is apparently simple to dress, present day and with no costume changes, there is always work to be done. At the most basic level, actors need someone to tidy up after them. They come off stage at the end of a performance, high on adrenaline and short on sense, scattering clothes in their haste to greet admiring friends in the foyer. If no one has the responsibility of returning everything to a hanger, no one will do it. Actors then arrive for the next performance to find that their tie, scarf, or shoe – and it is often only one shoe – is missing. Shirts and blouses may need laundering between performances – actors sweat and spill coffee on themselves in the interval. Clothes will need mending, there is always someone who pulls off a button, or stands on a hem.

In an amateur company, your wardrobe manager will usually be female and it is a bonus, though not essential, if she has a magic touch with a sewing machine. She needs to be organised, and like all crew, should be a calm and reassuring presence in the dressing room.

Responsibilities:

The main role of a wardrobe manager can be broken down into six areas:
1. To take the measurements of the cast, including hat, glove and shoe sizes where necessary.
2. To discuss the look of the play with the director and to establish a budget.
3. To do historical research where relevant.

4. To source all items of costume and arrange dates for collection and return of hired items.
5. To maintain the wardrobe during the show.
6. To arrange for the cleaning and return at the end of the run.

Listed like this, it sounds relatively simple, but never underestimate the potential problems she may encounter.

Costume that works

Discuss the costume requirements with your wardrobe mistress, talk to her about the overall impression that you want for each character. At this early stage don't be afraid to be very specific – colour, hemlines, style of hat, etc. – but if the ideal garment is not to be found, then be prepared to compromise. If you are intending to costume any of the technical crew, remember to add them to the list.

Actors need all the help they can get and the right costume can make an enormous contribution to their performance. As the director, you must use every means at your disposal to help the cast establish their characters and become that other person. It is therefore not a good idea to allow the cast to wear their own clothes – encourage them to at least borrow from a fellow actor instead.

Amateurs, from necessity, often wear their own shoes, but again, this is best avoided. The late Dame Wendy Hiller used to say that her performance was initially established once she found the right shoes. Loose fitting slippers, thigh length boots or six inch heels, for example, have a direct influence on the way we move and can have a greater impact on a performance than the actor's style of speech. Similarly, although they may not be aware of what is wrong, a shoe out of period will cast doubts in the mind of the audience – undisguised Doc Martins with distinctive yellow stitching are *not* a substitute for a Victorian boot. Simple black jazz shoes, on the other hand, can be ideal beneath medieval skirts. Judicious use of heels can also balance the height of actors; a tall woman playing opposite a shorter man should not wear heels!

Whilst on the subject of shoes, be aware of the noise they make. Working on a carpeted stage obviously solves the problem, but if your cast are literally 'treading the boards', leather soles and high heels can turn them into a herd of tap-dancing elephants. The solution is to stick felt or temporary rubber soles to the offending footwear.

Attention to detail is important for credibility. Finishing touches make all the difference and so jewellery comes under the wardrobe umbrella. Wedding rings on unmarried characters or missing from stage spouses can be easily overlooked and, like shoes, irritate the audience if a mistake slips through. Jewellery can even be dangerous. If the script requires a female actor to be slapped, check that she is not wearing earrings that are either heavy, sharp, or that could be accidentally caught – causing real pain, or worse, blood on a costume. Similarly, the actor who is inflicting the slap should not wear rings or bracelets that might do undue damage.

It is helpful if the actor is comfortable, but sometimes he, or more likely she, must suffer for their art. Corsets are by definition uncomfortable, but for Restoration plays, essential. Shoes that pinch a little, but look perfect, a jacket that looks good, but is a touch tight under the arms, may all have to be endured for a scene or two, but be reasonable and do not expect an actor to suffer throughout the whole play, they have enough to contend with. Nevertheless, there will be occasions when you will have to use your directorial authority and tell an actor to grin and bear it.

On the other hand, the agony can be very real, and completely accidental. Once, I appeared in a festival where time was of the essence. We had a 20 second change in between scenes and when the lights went up, I felt something was wrong and glanced down at my feet. The six inch, pointed stilettos had ended up on the wrong feet! Fortunately, the last act of *Steel Magnolias* involves little movement and a lot of tears – my tears were real by the end!

Anticipate problems

It is not sensible to spring surprises on your wardrobe mistress at technical rehearsal when she has little chance of sourcing a suitable replacement garment. Alert her early in rehearsals to potential problems.

If there is a struggle when the costume could be torn, then she must organise a back-up. When an item of clothing is to be torn deliberately, then she must work out the mechanics – loose tacking stitches and, of course, Velcro, which comes with its own ripping sound effect, can both work.

Does the script call for a spilt or thrown drink? If so, then the costume must be easily cleaned between performances and wardrobe would do well to keep a towel in the wings. Stage blood can be an absolute nightmare to wash out and it is worth experimenting with that type of stain. It may be possible for you to direct the scene so that the stain is confined to one piece of costume, but accidents do happen and it is prudent to organise for a substitute. When there is to be a matinee performance, then a second outfit can be essential. Unplanned spillages can be rescued with the magic of baby wipes, though always choose the 'sensitive' variety as some others are soapy.

Quick changes must also be discussed in advance. Ideally, the costume should be available at least a week, preferably two, before performance so that the change can be built into rehearsal. It is easier to remove clothing than to put it on and it may be possible for your character to underdress, wearing one outfit on top of another. Wardrobe must take care that the top clothing still appears to fit well and that outfit number two does not sneak out beneath the hem or a turn up. If underdressing is not an option, perhaps you can minimise the time required by adding or removing a jacket, changing a scarf or tie. It is surprising, but true, that whilst an audience will notice if a change is completely missing, it will happily accept such minor alterations.

When choosing an item required for a swift change, avoid hooks and eyes which become impossible in back stage gloom, buttons are little better. Instead, aim for zips – metal rather than plastic, which have a nasty habit of jamming – large poppers, and of course, Velcro. If none of these ploys are possible, arrange for the actor to have at least one dresser waiting in the wings. *Same Time Next Year* by Bernard Slade is a quick change nightmare, demanding that the two characters age five years between every scene. In our production, each actor had their own dresser, with an additional person to help with wigs, shoes and jewellery as required. The changes were built into the rehearsal schedule, and at performance came in at 30 seconds. However well you have rehearsed, actors can panic in performance and a good dresser must remain calm but firm. It is easy to forget the sequence of the change, e.g. shoes before trousers and the actor may require prompting. Your dresser should use single word cues, which the flustered performer can understand.

Bare essentials

There are plays which require the cast to appear in next to nothing. Some actors will have no problem with this, others can be self-conscious. It is often the case that the more left to the imagination, the sexier the image. So, instead of the traditional bra and pants of farce, your actress can wear a silky all-in-one teddy or a basque. Slinky dresses that threaten to slip downwards and expose more than they should can be tamed with double sided tape. Her male counterpart may feel more comfortable in boxers, rather than Y-fronts. For both sexes, it is a good idea to wear a second undergarment beneath the one exposed to the view of the audience and for gents in pyjamas, ask wardrobe to sew up the flies! It is important that your cast feel comfortable and therefore rehearse in a similar state of undress from an early stage so that it becomes second nature. Always tell them in advance and deal firmly with anyone who prevaricates – they took on the role and taking their clothes off is simply part of the job.

Total nudity on stage is unusual in amateur theatre, but where it cannot be avoided, it must be rehearsed. On the first occasion, it can be sensitive to work only with the actors involved until they are confident. Nudity must always serve the play, never detract – this is theatre and not sleaze. In *Dead Funny* by Terry Johnson, the leading man is required to strip and to remain on stage for a duologue with his wife. You want the audience to concentrate on their conversation without distractions, so think carefully about how you position him. It is usually done by allowing him to lie on the sofa with his wife strategically sitting in front of him, at his waist level. Even when fully clothed, actors risk exposure – in the literal sense of the word. A violent fight scene, or a character who dies on stage and is subsequently bundled off, needs to feel respectable and wardrobe should be alerted if bloomers and petticoats are likely to be visible. For a similar scene in a modern dress play, most actresses will have the sense to wear more than a thong!

Stage lights can play havoc with some fabrics, particularly white. Some white fabrics become almost transparent. Ultra-violet light will catch absolutely everything in its glare, so be extra vigilant. As always, anticipate the problem and deal with it before show week.

Colour

Costume can be used to subtly enhance the interpretation of a play and colour is an excellent tool. At its most basic level, the traditional white hat for good guy, black hat for bad guy still works, take it a stage further and consider whether colour can complement the personality of your character, red for tempestuous, sexy, blue for reserved, calm and so on. As mentioned earlier, white is difficult, not only can it become transparent, or luminous, it is generally difficult to light. Cream is an effective substitute. *Laying the Ghost* by Simon Williams, requires two characters to die and reappear as ghosts. The script calls for them to make their spectral appearance in white clothing identical to their previous outfit. We chose to put them in cream, and kept the 'live' clothes simple so that the illusion of transformation would be effective and credible.

Monochrome clothing with flashes of colour can also be interesting. In our production of *The Cocktail Party* by T. S. Eliot, we dressed the first act in black and cream, except for the three guardians who each had the same purple fabric incorporated into their costume, as a dress, as a tie and as a handkerchief, to indicate a relationship between them. Be creative, but aim to maintain a clear logic which will help the audience's understanding, too much of a good thing can be confusing and distracting.

We chose to make *The Cocktail Party* timeless, rather then setting it in 1950 when it was first published. Our costumes were a blend of classic elements borrowed from three eras, the 30s, 40s and 50s and it seemed to work.

A timeless production is one thing, but always strive to give the whole a coherent feel. A play which spreads across the centuries, without good reason, confuses the audience and looks chaotic rather than timeless. I have seen a Shakespearian production which included a 17th century shepherdess, a 1950s college professor, a scattering of Victorians and SS officers in black leather, and in my view, it simply did not work. If, however, your play is firmly anchored in a particular time, the wardrobe must hit the books and aim to be as accurate as possible. *A Man for All Seasons, Murder in the Cathedral, Crown Matrimonial*, to name but three, deal with a specific period in history, and will reap the benefit of careful research.

Sources

Budget is always a consideration, but in the case of a costume drama be realistic with your treasurer from the outset. It is not possible to do a full blown period piece without allowing a sensible amount of cash for costume hire. It is possible to obtain a costume by offering a mention, or an advert in the programme, but discuss this with publicity before making any promises.

Your company will have a list of local resources. This should include other nearby companies who may have a costume store, members who have case-loads of treasures in their attic – and don't forget the charity shops. If you cannot see what you want, always ask. Many such outlets have a collection of clothing that is too dated to be saleable, but perfect for theatre, squirrelled away in a back room.

Sourcing material for costumes that are to be specifically made for a production can be expensive if you are not careful. Check out local markets for reasonably priced fabric and haberdashery. Cheap fabric can look spectacular under lights. Lining material with a satin finish transforms into something rich and wonderful on a stage. Upholstery fabrics with contrasting threads or raised patterns are wonderful for opulent medieval-style costumes. In some areas, there are outlets that deal specifically in material for saris – these shops are always worth a visit. Again, charity shops can be the source of your perfect fabric – old curtains, bedspreads etc can all be transformed with a little ingenuity.

Rehearsal clothing

Costume dramas can bring another challenge for your cast, and again, do all you can to help them. Your actresses may need to learn how to manage something unfamiliar, like a dress with a six foot train, a bustle, or a corset. Handling long, heavy skirts, both walking in them and sitting down, must be practised if the actors are to feel comfortable and look credible. Arrange with your wardrobe manager to provide substitute practise skirts for rehearsals, even an underskirt will be a great help. Men do not completely escape the problem, and will need to learn how to handle a cloak, a top hat, and how to sit in a tail coat. A pantomime dame has a whole world of new clothes to deal with, and, although they may not thank you at the time, the sooner you push them into skirts, heels and bosoms, the better! Fat suits are rarely used, but having worn one myself, again, it is so helpful to get used to the way the padding alters your movements, particularly if, as in my case, the bust increases by several cup sizes!

Wardrobe management

As the items are sourced and approved, they should *all* be given to the wardrobe manager, who can then launder, mend, hang and label each item. Leaving pieces of costume in the hands of actors is dangerous – they can easily be left at home. If time allows, organise a costume parade before a rehearsal, about two weeks before the show. You may well have seen the clothing in ones and twos, but it is well worth reviewing the complete set of costume and checking that they look good together.

If there is to be a photo call, notify your wardrobe mistress in advance. Items which are being hired may not be available and she needs time to find something appropriate for the picture. Bear in mind that the majority of pictures only require head and shoulders, so discuss the details of the images required with your publicity manager and try to simplify her task.

All costumes should ideally be available the week before the show, at the very least, they must arrive in time for the technical rehearsal. As we said at the start of the chapter, the clothes will alter the way an actor behaves, and the more at home they feel as their character, the better.

From the start of show week, all the costumes should be hung on a rail in the dressing room, and clearly labelled with the name of the character and the scene. Label both the hanger and the costume. Use sellotape to 'laminate' the label on the hanger, or masking tape which seems to survive the ordeal of show week successfully. Ideally tack a strip of bias binding, marked with a laundry pen, to the inside of the costume. This is not always possible, and a piece of paper and a safety pin will have to do, but it is unlikely to survive more than one performance.

Nervous actors are careless with costumes, which end up strewn across the floor. Usually, with a small cast, wardrobe can cope, but with a large cast, the end result will be complete chaos. As the director, support your wardrobe manager if she has to read the riot act. It is not in the interests of a good production if vital bits of costume go missing and cause a last minute back stage panic. Make sure that any precious, hard to clean, easily torn items are pointed out to the cast.

The list

Wardrobe should create a comprehensive list of all items of costume – who they are for, where and when they come from, when and where they must be returned. (See appendix for a sample chart.) If this is not done, then there is a risk that a hire fee will be increased, a deposit withheld, or that a member of the group will lose something that has been lent. From experience, check through the items from any hired source, the descriptions are not always accurate. We borrowed about twenty straw hats from three different sources, but when it came to identifying the owners at the end of the show, the only description was – 'a straw hat'!

During the show

Starting with technical rehearsal, and throughout the week, wardrobe should arrive at least an hour before curtain up. All the elements of costume should be checked before the actors arrive, and set in the correct places, either on the costume rail, or laid out in the wings for a quick change. Always set costumes in the same place and the same order – it makes it easier for everyone to find and check.

The wardrobe mistress needs to bring a basic sewing kit for running repairs. I recommend she labels her scissors, which will otherwise disappear in to the stage manager's pockets or onto the props table. It may be useful to bring an ironing board and an iron. Without question, she must have a plentiful supply of safety pins of all shapes and sizes.

After every change, all costumes are returned to their appointed place and checked yet again at the end of the performance. This may sound pernickety, but it can save a lot of time the next evening, particularly if the wardrobe mistress is late arriving.

Strike

Take small and precious items away immediately after the last performance, the rest can wait. The remaining task is to sort the costumes into sets depending on their source and arrange for their safe return. This is when the master list becomes invaluable. It is very easy to forget where something has come from, even in a week. Some will need laundering or dry-cleaning and if they belong to a member of cast, it is good practice for the company to offer to pay the bill. The key trick for a wardrobe mistress is to not have random pieces of costume still in her boot a month later! And always check the pockets. It has been known for a wardrobe mistress to discover a current passport that had been used as a prop and then abandoned.

CHAPTER 9

Looking the Part

GOOD MAKE-UP is invisible. The magic of theatre is to create an illusion of reality and make-up should be used to serve that purpose. Once you become aware of it, the spell is broken. Make-up is a complex art and there are many good books on the subject if you want to develop this skill. The following comments are designed to point you in the right direction and avoid some of the common pitfalls.

The vast majority of productions need little, if any, make-up, but when it is used, 99% of the time the key rule is 'less is more'. No audience will take an actor seriously if he appears with an orange face and a few black smudges.

Make-up can be divided into three categories: straight, character and fantasy. **Straight make-up** is intended to enhance the features of the actor and to compensate for the bright lights and the distance from the audience. In every day communication we pick up many cues from the face, the expression in, and around the eyes and the mouth. We have a tendency to lip read, even if the person is standing next to us. There is a lot of truth in the phrase 'I can't hear properly without my glasses.' and since theatre is about communication, the make-up should be used to enable the audience to pick up the nuances of facial expression.

Men need the absolute minimum and can usually look fine with no make-up at all. The use of the old-fashioned No. 5 and 9 greasepaint should be avoided – it is tricky to apply, hot and sticky to wear and has a tendency to smudge. If you must use foundation, go for the modern water-based pancake. An actor whose skin looks unnaturally pale under lights does not necessarily need foundation and can be given a healthier glow by a touch of blusher. If the actor is fair, it may be worth adding emphasis to his eyebrows, and using a little mascara on the lashes, but don't go near him with eye liner or lipstick. For women, normal street make-up is usually enough, though you should take care that the make-up reflects the era of the play. When dealing with a chorus of ladies, provide a set of the same foundation and lip colour and aim for a uniform style.

Character make-up is exactly what it says, and should compliment the personality of the character, but keep it subtle, and credible. Aging an actor does not mean that their face should be covered with lines of dark purple 'lake' – shadows are often enough. Older skin tends to be pale, the eyelids take on a slightly pinkish look, the cheeks are hollow rather than plump, and the mouth is thinner. Transfer these ideas to your actor, by toning down their skin colour, avoiding blusher and adding a touch of pink-blue to the eye sockets. Eyebrows should not be given emphasis, indeed, the reverse, lighten them with a little foundation – brushing the hairs in the opposite direction from normal to produce a shaggy look can be remarkably effective.

If the actor is required to look considerably older than their years, then you may need to introduce facial lines. Use browns and sepia tones, never black, and follow the natural lines of the face, paying particular attention to the eyes. Lines work best if they are broken rather than solid. Often a face can be aged simply by the addition of highlights. If this is still not enough, then the highlights will help you decide which hollows need to be emphasised.

This process can take up to two hours on a 'new' face, so make time during the rehearsal period for your make-up artist to practise and become accustomed to her canvas – do not expect her to be able to 'read' the face and produce the desired effect first time.

Fantasy make-up is in a league of its own. It is not too difficult to create an exotic look for genies, fairies and dancers, but people acting as animals need an experienced hand on the brush. Animals also have a tendency to come in herds, so you need to find yourself a practised team of artists who are both accurate and fast.

Theatre make-up, brushes and cosmetic sponges are not cheap, so make allowance in the budget for the equipment you are going to need. Your make-up artist is also responsible for keeping the kit in good order and most importantly, for maintaining good hygiene. When actors are responsible for their own make-up, attempt to train them to return everything they borrow to the make-up table. This rarely works, so appoint a specific individual, probably the wardrobe mistress, to tidy the kit and wash all brushes and sponges after every performance.

Hair

Facial hair should be treated with caution. Day job permitting, it is always best if the actor can grow his own. It is possible to buy ready-made moustaches and such like, but these will need trimming and fitting to the actor if they are to look natural. Again, allow time for experimentation before technical rehearsal. Your make-up artist should check that there is no allergic reaction to the glue she intends to use and the actor will benefit from rehearsing in the whiskers – moustaches can be difficult to come to terms with! If you have someone with the relevant skills, it is cheaper to buy false hair and make your own from scratch. The hair comes in a tightly twisted plait which must be undone and straightened. In the past, I have spent hours over a pan of hot water, steaming the kinks out, but these days a steam iron on a low setting does the job a lot faster. Then, rather than simply cutting a suitable chunk directly from the newly straightened hair, tease out sections with a fine comb, and reshape them into the side-burn or moustache.

The hair can be attached with spirit gum, specifically designed for the purpose and it is worth adding the specific glue-remover to your shopping list. Rubber solution glue can also work but is not as skin-friendly. Hair and wigs can work a magic transformation, so much so, that make-up can become redundant. For example, in *Same Time Next Year* the couple age 25 years during the performance and there is no time between scenes for a complicated make-up job. The female character can be transformed by wigs, the man by changing his hair style – tousled, slicked back, different parting, perhaps add a touch of grey to the temples between the acts. The change of hair, coupled with the way the characters move, is enough to create the illusion of passing years.

Greying hair and eyebrows can add years to a face. Talcum powder used to be a popular method for amateurs, but this dulls the hair, leaves your actor with a heavy case of dandruff and looks like … talcum powder! There are a range of sprays on the market that will give a much better end result. As a last resort, a dab of white pancake, or even white liquid shoe cleaner can work, provided they are applied sparingly.

Wigs need to be firmly anchored if the actor is to move naturally. It helps to either use a net over their own hair, or better still, make a skull cap from a pair of old tights to use as a non-slip base. It is worth spending a reasonable amount of money on a good quality wig – it can always go into the group's stock and cheap ones never look right. Wigs benefit from being treated with respect, and kept on a block when not in use.

Hair styles, like costume and make-up, should be historically accurate. For a play set in the 30s or 40s, you may have the job of persuading your male cast to have a short back and sides. The most drastic request that I have ever had to make, was to persuade a teenage boy with hair half-way down his back, to have it cut for the role of Adrian Mole who could not be seen with flowing locks! For women, period hair styles need to be researched and tried out before show week.

CHAPTER 10

The Props Table

STAGE PROPERTIES OR 'props', is the term that covers practically everything on the set that is not nailed down – from the pictures on the walls to the contents of a handbag. Much of the work is done well before the week of performance and often other members of the team can be unaware of just how many hours this role can take up, not to mention the number of miles that can be travelled in search of an elusive item.

The responsibilities of a property manager are deceptively straightforward:

1. Make a list of all relevant items, source them and arrange for them to be delivered.
2. Supply the cast with personal props during rehearsals that are as close to the real thing as possible.
3. Check that all props are in their appointed place before the performance.
4. Check that each actor has her/his personal props.
5. Plan and execute set changes with the stage manager.
6. Organise a props table.
7. Maintain the props in good order and return them at the end of the show.

However, beneath this list lies a whole host of challenges. The following will give you a taste of some of the more common problems that she may have to deal with.

Planning the list

Many acting editions include a list of required items at the back of the book. Whilst this is a valuable guide, it is not necessarily exhaustive. Ideas for additional items are likely to occur to you as you block and work the scenes, others may become redundant, so keep a separate sheet of paper specifically for props notes. If you decide that a particular scene works well with a rain sound effect, should you add an umbrella? Is it a good idea to let a character knit, crochet or embroider? Props managers often do not attend the first few rehearsals, so make sure you keep her well informed of any changes. She will not thank you if she has been scouring the country for an item that is no longer wanted.

Furniture

The historical period of the play dictates the style of the furnishings. Even if you decide that the overall design should be timeless, give props some clues as to the general style that you envisage. Think about the size of the furniture – do you really have room for an enormous three-seater sofa or will a small two-seater suffice? The set design should provide an idea of the amount of stage space and if you have a major set change, don't forget to take account of the extent, or lack of, wing space that is available for storage.

The colour of the set is also a factor. There are times when the final shade of paint or wallpaper is chosen to fit the furniture that has been begged or borrowed, but if you have firm views, props needs to know.

On the subject of borrowing, be careful not to cajole a friend into lending you something that is either precious or breakable – accidents do happen. If you borrow curtains or upholstered furniture, always get the owner's permission to fire proof the article.

Sofas

Sofas are often the hardest item to source and an item which will result in a compromise between what you want and what you can have. It is often possible to put something the right size and shape, but totally the wrong colour into 'costume'. Throws and cushions may be enough, or you may wish to give the thing a complete new look with temporary re-upholstery. This is not as hard as it sounds – remember it is only seen from a distance, and most of the back and perhaps one side is often completely hidden from the audience. A few tacking stitches, safety pins and/or a staple gun to keep the fabric taut and you can achieve the desired effect in a remarkably short time, but always, always, always, get permission from the owner before attacking someone's prized possession in this way.

Before finally deciding on a sofa or arm chair, check that the cast can sit and stand with relative ease. Some furniture is so low that cast disappear into the cushions and have a major struggle to get up again. It may be that the cast simply have to learn to deal with it, but do your best to make life easier for them. Sometimes the problem can be solved by hiding extra padding, like a duvet or a sheet of wood beneath the top cushions.

Beds

Beds are another space-eating item, particularly the double kind, but appearances can be deceptive. Sometimes it is only necessary to have the foot of the bed showing, and then you can create the illusion with a suitably draped box. *Same Time Next Year* by Bernard Slade demands a double bed, but we convinced our audience with a generous single, placed at a strategic angle. When much of the action takes place around a bed, for example, *A Kind of Alaska* by Pinter, *Conversations With a Golliwog* by Alexander Guyan or *Whose Life is it Anyway* by Bryan Clark, it is helpful to audience and cast if the head of the bed is raised to offer better sight lines.

Cars
Not strictly furniture, but the biggest prop we ever had to handle was a Mini for Alan Ayckbourn's *Just Between Ourselves*. After reassuring ourselves, and the venue, that that the stage could take the weight, we removed the engine, and replaced it with a lightweight replica. It raised more than a few eyebrows as it was carried in! In the same play, all the back stage paraphernalia that was used to build the set stayed on stage to make the perfect dressing for the garage shelves.

Glass

Pictures and mirrors can be a nightmare for lighting. Glass can be toned down with hair lacquer or polish, but this usually gives a patchy result so think very carefully where you put them and adjust the angle at which they hang to minimise reflection and glare.

Food and drink

Eating and drinking on stage is always exciting for the actors, the least that props can do is to ensure that the items that must actually be consumed are edible. Props should be made aware of any serious pet hates among the cast, and more seriously should be alerted to allergies or medical conditions such as diabetes, and adjust the menu accordingly.

In early rehearsals, it is fine for the cast to mime pouring a cup of tea, or a drink, but in the final runs it is important that they use actual liquid – water will do. The weight of a full cup and saucer is quite different, the time it takes to open a bottle and pour a drink is probably not what the actor imagined, and finally, you cannot wave your arms about in gay abandon with a full glass! Many amateur productions are marred by empty teapots pouring air, so always, always, pour something, preferably resembling the real thing.

Apple juice or flat dry ginger can masquerade as whisky, blackcurrant squash can imitate red wine and white wine can be simulated by using one of the herbal cordials on the market, water will cover for gin and vodka.

When serving hot food or drinks, keep an eye on the temperature. A steaming cup may look good, but scalding the cast will not be appreciated.

Always keep food apart from other props to avoid accidental contamination in the back stage gloom. There was a memorable performance of *Lady Winder-mere's Fan*, where the ink, fortunately created from blue food colouring, became confused with the milk and the consequence was blue milk and murky green tea!

Glasses that are carried in on a smart silver tray have a nasty tendency to slip, particularly when in the hands of an inexperienced waiter. If they are never actually removed from the tray, stick them down with blu-tack, if they are to be used, a touch of double sided tape may give extra security.

Fresh food does not stay fresh for long under stage lights and the budget should allow for new stock during the run. If an item in question is never actually eaten and will therefore last for the week of the show, just be careful that some actor does not take a bite of it on the last night.

Flowers and plants

It is worth using real flowers where you can. Although they will not wilt, plastic blooms look plastic and are a fire hazard. Plants and shrubs can become very thirsty under stage lights so it should be part of the props team's routine to water them each evening, preferably after the performance to avoid accidental spillage. Flowers can be used to suggest mood. A single faded bloom could indicate sadness, whereas an opulent colourful bunch can reflect wealth and contentment.

Personal props

Personal properties are the items that an actor needs about his person, such as photographs, handbag contents, cigarettes, handkerchiefs and such like. They tend to be small, vital to the action and easily lost. Your props manager should insist that these items remain in the theatre between performances and should be double checked each evening.

Rehearsal props

For blocking purposes, use the furniture that you have available in the rehearsal room to represent the finished set. Piano stools make effective coffee tables, two chairs placed side by side can pretend to be a sofa.

Once the basic moves are in place, your props manager should be expected at rehearsals to provide the next layer of detail. She can then be kept well informed of any alterations to her list, and begin to get the shape of the play – where the props changes come, what needs to be done, when she is required in the wings to give or receive trays.

Props, such as handbags and glasses, or more likely, plastic cups, are invaluable in the early stages. Without some physical representation it is remarkably hard to keep track of who put what down where.

Setting up

All properties should arrive at the theatre during the final set-up and be stored safely, well away from the frenetic activity on stage. Remember that the stage is controlled by the stage manager, or set builder, and props must wait for permission before placing anything on stage. Jump the gun at this time and you run the risk of props being broken.

When the furniture has been arranged to everyone's satisfaction, the stage manager should arrange for the positions to be taped. Props should also liaise with the stage manager so that all relevant fabrics are sprayed with fire retardant.

The props table

The property manager should discuss the siting of her table with the stage manager, particularly if anything that can be spilled or broken is involved. Any old table will do, provided that it does not wobble! It is good practice to mark the table with masking tape into sections for each item, and to write the name of the object on the tape. It is then easier to check that everything is present and correct and to return the item to the same place each night.

Set changes

If the property manager and her team have been attending rehearsals, they should be familiar with the requirements of each scene change. It is not enough to tell them what needs to be done – each member of the team should be given a specific task or tasks or else you risk some key item being forgotten. She should take into consideration the layout of the venue, check the available entrances on the set plan, and know which side the props table is likely to be. She should also be looking for short cuts in the interest of speed. So, if she must clear a table laid with a cloth and a few unbreakable items, it may save precious seconds to simply bundle everything into the cloth, rather than remove each item separately.

However, working in rehearsal conditions and fumbling about in the semi-darkness back stage are two different things, so make sure to give them time to rehearse changes during the technical rehearsal.

Many back stagers will run a mile rather than act, but, if the set changes are to be done in full view of the audience, it is worth considering whether to put them into costume or not. At the very least, the team should be dressed in stage-crew black with quiet shoes. There are a good number of plays that will allow you to dress your props manager as a maid or a butler, a cleaner or a removal man – you get the idea. This has the advantage of making the set change part of the play, it can be done faster because you can use a brighter lighting state and it gives the audience something to watch.

Strike

This should run in the reverse order from set up and the property manager should be one of the first on the scene. All small items should be removed from the stage and the props table cleared, before taking down drapes and removing furniture.

Props must then check everything against her list and organise the safe, and clean, return of each borrowed item.

CHAPTER 11

Let There Be Light!

LIGHTING IS AN essential ingredient of theatre magic, yet it is often sadly neglected. Many amateur directors are technophobic and prefer to leave the cables and sockets to someone else. This section will not turn you into an electrician, but should give you some idea of what lighting can do for your production and the vocabulary to communicate with your technicians.

Why lighting?

The obvious reason is to illuminate the stage and focus the attention of the audience on the performance. Lighting is also essential in creating the location and mood of a scene. Then, if you feel really creative, it can be used to underline dramatic moments.

Good lighting completes the illusion of reality and the audience will take it for granted. Bad lighting on the other hand, detracts from the performance and will provoke comment.

Lighting the stage sounds easy, but it is not enough to hang a few lanterns and point them at the stage. Even the simplest of lighting plans takes forethought and skill from your designer. The lamps, or lanterns as they are sometimes called, have to be positioned so that there are no dark corners or shadows, unless of course the play specifically requires such an effect. Remember, shadows can be cast by props and actors in the wings, as well as on stage. Hotspots – areas that are brighter than the rest of the stage – are just as bad as shadows and should be eliminated. Finally, plain white light is usually too harsh and can wash out the features of the actors, so some form of coloured gel is usually required.

The majority of plays will use a permutation of four basic types of lighting state.

1. Interior daylight

Pretty straightforward, but if you have a window with a backing flat, don't forget to light that too.

2. Interior night time

To create the effect of artificial light, consider using warmer tones and a lower level of brightness. If you have practical lamps on stage, you may wish to 'help' the effect by assigning a lamp to exaggerate the light thrown by the real thing. This can be particularly effective if your play calls for oil lamps or candles. You may choose to use a moonlight wash to suggest darkness. This is a convention that an audience will readily accept for either indoor or outdoor lighting.

3. Outdoor settings

Your designer has to take the time of day and the weather into account.

4. Darkness

Some productions call for a scene to take place with no apparent source of light at all while requiring the audience to follow the action. Experiment with low levels, but don't make the stage so dark that not only can the audience see nothing, but the cast will fall over the furniture!

It is not always possible, or desirable, to use curtains to signal the end of a scene and lighting will provide your punctuation and cover any changes. Again, ensure that your crew can see enough to do their job safely and efficiently.

There are two other lighting tasks to be considered.

1. Lighting the auditorium

Many groups use the normal lighting of the hall or theatre, but you can do better. Subdued light immediately separates the theatre from the everyday world and creates an air of anticipation. So if you have the resources ask for a couple of lanterns to be rigged specifically to light your venue, pointing them upwards and bouncing the light from the ceiling can be very effective. At the very least, do not turn on every light in the hall. Provided there is enough light for the audience to see seat numbers and read their programmes they will be happy.

Finally, as a Health and Safety requirement, all illuminated exit signs must be in full working order.

2. Back stage lighting

The stage area will have some form of everyday lighting, apart from the lights that are controlled from the board, that are referred to as 'workers'. This working light is usually too bright and too white to be suitable for use during a show and should be switched off. Lighting for set changes that take place behind the curtains should be controlled from the board. You can afford to be a little brighter than for changes that take place in full view of the audience, but not much.

The back stage area and the wings should be dimly lit so that your team can work safely. Blue bulbs are ideal for the purpose, failing that, cover any back stage light source with blue gel.

Location, location, location

A large majority of plays have a single location and call for nothing more than for the actors to be visible. Other productions, Shakespeare being the most obvious example, require the lighting to provide the scenery and reflect the mood of the scene.

Create an instant wood, or a prison cell by using a gobo. Gobos are a metal stencil placed in a profile lantern which produces a hard light that can be focussed. These gadgets can produce a vast range of patterns. There is also a range of gobos that move and flicker, giving the effect of fire or water, for example.

You can also make use of projected images, both still and moving, to enhance your production. My own group cast a fireworks sequence onto the ceiling and wall above the proscenium arch and when coupled with sound, the effect was almost like the real thing.

The most obvious way of creating atmosphere is by use of coloured gels. Whilst pale colours are most commonly used, stronger tones have their own magic. Red gives a passionate feel, blue is calmer and used to give an impression of night, oranges and yellows are warm and sunny and green is best kept for theatrical apparitions. Colours can be changed during performance by using scrollers. These devices roll the gel colour of your choice into position, but be warned, they can be noisy.

Be creative

Lighting can create a mood, but can also be used to underline the action of the play, shifting the audience's attention to a specific actor or an important speech. Spotlights are normally confined to musical productions, but have their uses in straight drama. Dropping the surrounding light and bringing a spot onto a solo actor will immediately focus the attention of the audience, during a soliloquy, for example. Adding an extra spotlight on top of the current lighting state has a similar effect and could be used to isolate one actor while others remain on stage. Dimming the main lighting, focusing into a pool of light, which itself slowly fades, is perfect for a down-beat ending.

In our production of *The Cocktail Party* by T. S. Eliot we used lighting as an integral part of the setting. Working with the designer, we created a set entirely from muslin drapes and set a number of lights, gelled with three different colours, on the floor behind them. In the first act, when the characters are in a state of change and uncertainty, the set was mainly back-lit and as characters came and went, the colours were shifted. In the final act, where life is more settled, the coloured back light was abandoned in favour of more conventional lighting from the front.

Lights, like actors, need to have a reason to move and change. They may alter when a new character enters or with a variation in conversation. Finally, if you pick your moment to team a shift in illumination with the introduction of music, you have an emotionally powerful combination.

Talk to your lighting technician early in the rehearsal process so that he is aware of the set design and your concept of the play. Omit this preliminary consultation at your peril – there is nothing worse than discovering at technical rehearsal that a vital effect has been made impossible because there is a flat in the way. Conversely, you may be offered ideas that you had never considered.

Tools of the trade

Lights come in a variety of shapes and sizes. Each lamp is hung with a bracket and must also have a safety chain. Some will have shutters or flaps known as barn doors, to allow the designer to control the width of the beam. It is not essential for a director to know which lamp does what. Your only concern is that it works for you, but the following basic terminology may help you feel less of a foreigner!

1. Flood

This is the simplest type of lamp with no lens and no adjustment. The symmetric variety produce a general wash of light and are often used as temporary houselights. The asymmetric floods are known as cyc floods and are invaluable in lighting the backdrop, or cyclorama.

2. Fresnel

The fresnel, pronounced 'frennel', is a soft-edged spotlight, offering more control over the size of the beam angle than floods. The beam can be shaped by using barn doors. The light is named after the French inventor Augustin Jean Fresnel who developed the concentric ridged lens for use in lighthouses.

Fresnels are one of the simplest ways to produce an even wash of colour across the stage using the fewest number of lanterns.

3. Parcans

Parcans are relative latecomers to the lighting designers' armoury and were first used for rock concerts in the 70s. They are cheap, weigh little and are capable of emitting an intense beam.

4. PC spots

Pebble convex spotlights have a slightly harder edge to the light than fresnels.

5. Profiles

These produce clearly defined areas of light which can be focussed and are perhaps the most versatile of all. These are the only lanterns that can be used with a gobo to project an image onto the stage floor or the set.

6. Follow spots

As indicated by their name, follow spots can track a performer across the stage and are usually manually controlled.

Other names, such as harmony, quartet and nocturne may be banded about. Do not panic, these are simply brand names and not a different breed. As a rough guide, profile lanterns have shutters and/or an iris for controlling the light, whilst fresnels have barn doors.

Lights are usually rigged in pairs, one on either side of the stage, so that the finished effect is balanced. A word of caution – check that your stage is central to the auditorium. My group moved into a newly built venue, the lighting technicians set up a basic rig, turned on the lights and realised that the stage was a couple of metres off-centre – so we had to start again!

The lights are plugged into a numbered socket which corresponds with a number assigned to it on the lighting board. The board can be manual or computer controlled and although at first sight it appears fiercely complicated, remember it is all done by numbers. Each sliding switch matches a light, or pair of lights, and moving it up and down controls the brightness – not difficult. Manual boards are completely within the operator's control, allowing for 'live' adjustments. This is particularly handy if your errant cast decide to miss a few pages. A computer board which can be pre-programmed has the advantage of being easier to operate, on the other hand it is more difficult to adjust when things go wrong.

The rig is fed from dimmer packs – giant resisters which adjust the power supply. You may hear your electricians talking about 'patching' – this is the process of spreading the available current evenly to avoid overloading and tripping the system. It is also where lights are paired up i.e. plugged into one channel on the dimmer pack, in order to be operated by one fader on the lighting desk. This is a handy technique if you are working with a limited number of channels.

Avoiding problems

Fuses can trip and bulbs may blow, and worst case scenario, you could have a power cut, but some problems can be minimised with a little forethought. When using a hired venue, ask your lighting technician to arrange a visit about ten days before the get-in. He can then check the equipment while there is still time for any faults to be rectified, and to order any supplementary lights should that prove necessary. He should also find out if there is an adequate supply of spare bulbs on site.

Always check any appliance that you take in with you. Many venues will not allow you to import anything electrical, but if they do, check it out. A dress rehearsal was once plunged into darkness because of a faulty kettle – you have been warned!

CHAPTER 12

Sound Practice

SOUND IS SOMEHOW not as foreign a concept as lighting to the technically challenged. All you as a director need to worry about is what sound you want, what direction it should come from, and how loud it should be.

Live is best

Not every sound effect needs to be recorded, in many cases, it is far better to do it live – take doors for example. Numerous plays have front doors that open and close off stage, they call for bells, or knockers and the sound of keys in the lock. If you do not own one already, it is well worth constructing a door box for these effects. This is simply a box, which gives added resonance to the sound, about a metre high, that has a solid door, complete with a solid domestic catch. Attach a battery-run doorbell to the top, a knocker to the side and there you have it. The sound of keys rattling is sufficient to indicate locking and unlocking. There is no point in adding a working lock to your box, the keys will disappear and finding a key hole in the gloom of the wings is not recommended. The box can be operated by the stage crew, but the timing is usually better if the actors to do it themselves.

Telephones that ring from somewhere ten feet away always grate, no matter how good your recording. It is best to find an instrument that has a working ring and to arrange for sound to connect it into the system.

The sound of breaking glass or china never sounds quite right on a recording. Experiment, in the theatre, with breaking things into a metal bucket – stage managers can find this therapeutic!

Spoken announcements within the context of the play are also better done from a microphone in the wings, for example, the voice of the computer in *Deadly Embrace*. Gun shots, made by using a starting pistol in the wings are also more effective than effects. Live sound gives flexibility in the event of mistakes. There is a sound sequence at the end of *The Ghost Train*, the approaching train, gun shots and so on. At one performance of this play, the actor gave the cue line to start the tape, and then happily jumped half a page, forcing the panic struck prompter to hiss 'The gun, the ******* gun!' until the actor regained his wits.

Other effects have to be pre-recorded, such as bird song, traffic, rain and thunder. This type of effect is now easy to obtain on specially compiled CDs.

There are three main ranges of sound effects available. BBC, Digifex and Bits and Pieces that can be ordered from technical suppliers such as Canford Audio or Lancelyn. Do not simply ask your sound person for the sound of rain, and hope for the best – get hold of them and listen for yourself. These CDs offer the luxury of choosing from a surprising variety of recordings. Do you want heavy rain, a light shower, rain on an open window, on a closed window, on the roof of a car? As director, your job is to create the illusion of reality on the stage and well chosen sound effects can make a real difference.

On the subject of illusion and credibility, it is important that the sound seems to come from a logical direction. If the bird song is supposed to be heard through the up stage right window, then that is where the speaker should be. When it is supposedly raining and an actor enters from outside, aim to raise the volume of the rain effect to indicate the opening of the door. Discuss your requirements with your sound technician, and establish the feasibility of placing speakers where you want them. As with all your crew, this conversation should not be left to the last minute. Some venues only have auditorium speakers, so if you want to have sounds coming from behind the actors, your technician needs time to arrange for additional speakers.

Music

It is music that sets the tone of the evening before the curtain opens. The theme that you choose to open the performance can be one of the most important directorial decisions that you take. The key and tempo should match with the mood of the play – comedies tend to do best with up-beat melodies in a major key, while heavy dramas will suit slower music that is written in a minor key. Using songs that have appropriate lyrics can be fun, for example 'A bicycle made for two' could work for *When We Are Married*, while 'Let's face the music and dance' worked for *The Cocktail Party*. Listen to your chosen piece and find a suitable point to raise the curtain. This will probably be somewhere around 60–90 seconds into the music.

You can choose to keep the same piece for curtain up on the next act, or acts, on the other hand if there is a clear mood change, use something different. When making your selection, bear in mind that music can be a signpost to the audience, hinting at how they are expected to feel, and suggesting what may be about to happen.

Music is invaluable in covering scene changes. Never leave your audience in a dark and silent auditorium, they will become restless. Even with music, set changes should be done in under 30 seconds. Again, you may repeat the opening, or choose something different. Whatever your choice, always ask for more to be recorded than you need. The final decision is whether to fade the music out, or simply stop the recording, Both options have a place, but as a general rule, if in doubt, go for a fade.

Sometimes it can be very effective to continue with the music after the lights go up, but to transfer the sound so that it appears to come from a radio, or gramophone on the stage. If you take this route, be careful about the technicalities of incidental and interpolated music which are discussed in the chapter on theatre and the law.

As a lateral thought, the spoken word can be effective between scenes. If you take this route, then it is logical to let the poem or passage take its course from beginning to end, otherwise, those members of the audience who have actually been listening can feel cheated.

Increasingly, music is being used in the theatre in the same way as in films and television, to underscore the action and, or, the dialogue. In some ways, this is not new, but a return to Victorian melodramas. There are those who find underscoring a complete anathema, but used with care, this technique can add that extra something to your production. Music, particularly when combined with lights, is a potent tool for creating atmosphere and emotion. Choose your pieces with great care, a bad choice will do far more harm than good. Unless you are going for a deliberate effect, avoid anything that includes the lyrics, and use something that is unfamiliar. Take a CD player to rehearsals and experiment before making the final selection. That way, you can establish whether the piece complements your actor, where best to fade in and fade out, and as a final bonus, the actor becomes accustomed to working with music in the background.

Music is also used as a background while the audience are taking their seats and during the interval. Few people will actually listen to it, but aim to use something appropriate.

Even if your sound plot is basic, with music for the opening, a set change or two and at the end of the play, whoever is to operate the board must attend at least one rehearsal of a full run, excluding technical rehearsal. With more complex plots, the number of rehearsals they attend should increase appropriately.

Communication

When lights and sound are working from the back of the auditorium, the sound technician will be responsible for organising a means of communication between the control box and the stage manager. It is also very helpful to rig some means by which the cast can hear what is happening on stage. Systems vary widely, but if your dressing room is close to the stage, a standard baby listener will do the job.

Musicals

Musicals make heavy demands on sound. Rather than blind you with science, the best advice is to find a sound technician who really understands about microphones, levels and balancing. The vocalists must be balanced with the live band, orchestra, or recording and are likely to need some form of amplification. The chorus can be covered with stationary mics either at the front of the stage or above their heads. Soloists will need an extra boost. This will take you into the world of hand-held and radio mics, which can be a minefield of technical jargon.

Among the key things that a director should know is that radio mics operate on different frequencies, otherwise they will interfere with each other. Even two on different, but similar, frequencies can cause problems. If this happens, and there is a sudden stream of unpleasant screaming noises, don't panic, but be patient while the problem is resolved. This can involve checking every mic and can take time. This equipment often runs on batteries, and batteries run out faster than you think. If you run a dress rehearsal on the same day as a performance, check whether there will be sufficient time to recharge the units, and always have a supply of spare batteries in the wings. You should also check that there is a supply of microporous tape in the wings, which is ideal for securing the head sets to the actors.

Technical problems aside, you may need to adjust your blocking to accommodate the kit. Mics that are shared need to end up of the correct side of the stage for the next performer's entrance, and if the crew do not have time to run a mic from one side of the stage to the other you will have to do a swift re-think.

CHAPTER 13

Front of House

THE FRONT OF house manager is the public face of the company. He is responsible for the comfort and welfare of the audience from the moment they set foot in the theatre. His task begins two or three weeks before the show, when he can begin to assemble a team for each night. The exact number required will vary according to the anticipated size of audience and the style of the venue, but all the following front of house posts need to be filled:
1. Box office
2. Programme sellers
3. Ushers
4. Bar/coffee staff

The front of house team are not there for the odd half hour to sell programmes or tickets and then go home. They should remain for the duration of the show and be immediately available in the event of an emergency. It is important that all front of house staff are identifiable to the audience. The recommended dress code is formal black and white, for both sexes. The staff are then not only easy to spot, but they can convey an air of elegance and occasion which will put your audience in the mood for an evening out. For this reason, polo shirts, or similar clothing that bears the group logo is not really suitable, and best restricted to the technical crew.

Bar and refreshments

When there is to be a bar at a venue that does not habitually have such a facility, it is essential to apply for a license to sell alcohol and the application must be made well in advance. The local magistrates court will advise on procedure, but the sittings to approve occasional licenses are usually on a monthly basis and you do not want to miss the boat. It saves time and trouble if you can apply for a season's worth of licenses in one go, always assuming you have booked your venue and know the precise dates.

When the audience is going to contain a large number of under-18's, the court normally insist that soft drinks and alcohol are sold from two different areas. The official piece of paper should be displayed near the bar on the night and the person whose name is on the license must be present. It is acceptable to have an under-18 serving coffee and tea, but under no circumstances can they serve alcohol.

The manager should check that glasses and bar stock, coffee, tea etc, have been ordered and that collection has been arranged. Keep the bar stock simple. Red and white wine, two types of fizzy drink, and perhaps, orange juice. Wine is best bought on a sale-or-return basis and many retailers and supermarkets will happily do this. Most outlets will offer free hire of glasses alongside your purchase. Beer and lager cans are best avoided. The cans are bulky to store, you will probably sell fewer than you expect and since they are usually sold in multi-packs, you will only be able to return packs that have not been broken into. The price list should be agreed with the treasurer and prominently displayed.

Whether you choose to sell alcohol or not, it is always worth offering tea and coffee. China crockery is always preferable, but if you must use disposable cups, go for the more expensive polystyrene variety. The audience will not appreciate burnt fingers. Again, display a price list.

Float

The front of house manager should also liase with the treasurer to ensure that programmes, box office and refreshments have a float. Use your common sense and adjust the coinage to the change that you are likely to have give i.e. if programmes are 50p then that is what your sellers will need.

Box office

The box office procedure will have been organised by either the publicity manager and/or the permanent staff of a hired venue. It is the front of house manager's job to oversee the process, so the audience move from street to seats with the minimum of fuss and delay.

If you have space in the foyer, you can speed the process by having a separate area for pre-booked tickets that have been paid for. Use an old shoe box and file the tickets in alphabetical order. If your tickets are hard to read, it is worth taking the time to sort them into labelled envelopes. This table should not handle cash of any kind. Those people who have bothered to reserve a place are entitled to be given special treatment.

Then have a second point for those who have ordered tickets, but need to pay and for customers who wish to buy them on the night. If you only have one box office point, it is still worth separating the pre-paid tickets.

Double bookings do happen and whether the box office is managed by the venue or the group, the front of house manager should be on hand to solve the problem and soothe the ruffled customer. First check the date and the venue – people have been known to turn up on the wrong night, and even for an entirely different show!

Programme sellers

It is advisable to have at least two people for even the smallest of venues to avoid queues. Each seller must have:
  a supply of programmes
  a small bag for the money
  a float

Ushers

Again at least two people, preferably three. Position one usher, who can also sell programmes, by the entrance to the auditorium to indicate where the seat is located and which route provides the easiest access. The other two can direct people to the precise seat and give assistance to elderly or disabled customers. Those working in the auditorium should be armed with torches. When the show is running, they should sit at the back of the auditorium in case there are any problems. At the interval, they need to open and close the doors for the audience.

Warning notices

A show that uses strobe lighting *must* display a notice to that effect in the foyer. Some individuals are sensitive to the flashing light and can have an epileptic attack as a direct result.

It is also a good idea to have the following posters prominently displayed: 'Please switch off your mobile'; 'No Flash Photography or Video Recording'. These warnings should be repeated verbally immediately before the perform-ance starts. Mobile phones that ring during performance are infuriating to audience and cast alike. The unexpected flash of a camera may go unnoticed by the audience, but it can be completely off-putting for an actor. More importantly, there are clear legal reasons why performances may not be photographed or videoed.

The sound technician can arrange for a recorded message that can be played routinely when the house lights dim and you have the audience's attention. For example: 'Ladies and gentlemen, welcome to the Limelight Theatre. Please switch off all mobile phones. We would remind you that photography and video recordings are not permitted. Thank you.'

Despite all these warnings, it is not uncommon for someone to sneak in a camera, particularly if children are involved. If this should happen, it is down to the FOH manager to identify the culprit and to speak to them, politely, but firmly at the earliest opportunity. Those carrying video cameras are easier to spot on their way into the auditorium. Again, these individuals should be approached politely, and, if you have the facilities, offer to store their camera in a secure place during the performance.

Seat numbering

Your company may be fortunate and operate in a venue with numbers that are permanently attached to the seats. Be warned, these numbers can drop off with time, so always check that your ushers are familiar with the layout so that they can, literally, fill in the gaps. If you are working with individual chairs, with no numbers, be creative, but be clear. Taping the row letter to the floor by the appropriate aisle is a good strategy. The individual seats can be labelled by hand – written stickers, or tie-on labels. Whatever method you use, if this is your regular venue do try and develop a system that is re-usable.

It is also worth creating 'Reserved' signs, for VIP's and the press. It will make them feel special, and they can find their seat with the minimum of fuss. Even with numbered seats, it is all too easy for someone to sit in the wrong place and give you an embarrassing moment. When you know in advance that you have a disabled patron who needs a specific seat, again, do them the courtesy of marking their place. These notices are vital if you are working to a system of unreserved seating.

On the night and safety issues

The front of house manager should arrive an hour before curtain up at the latest. He should check that pre-booked tickets are available, that refreshments are in order, the float is on hand and that the programmes have actually made it to the venue.

Apart from catering for the comfort of the audience, the manager is also responsible for safety. Technically, the overall manager of the venue will have the ultimate responsibility, but sometimes the task falls completely on front of house. It is important to understand the responsibilities that accompany the specific building that you are working in, since they will vary to some degree.

Whether there is a legal requirement or not, a good manager will make a check of fire exits before the audience arrives. There should be no obstruction attached to a fire door; no chains, padlocks, or pieces of string and, obviously, they should not be locked. There must be clear access on both sides of the door. In the case of an exit which leads onto a car park, it is worth making sure that some bright spark, usually a late-comer, has not parked directly in front of the 'Fire Exit Keep Clear' sign and believe me, they do. All illuminated exit signs must be working.

Fire doors must be able to close easily – again, no obstructions, door stops, etc. One venue in which my group have worked has a particularly noisy fire door between dressing room and stage. Unless closed very, very slowly, it crashes shut with a thud. Tying a tea-towel around the handles to muffle the noise is not acceptable. You must either train your cast and crew to be super-careful, or, have a door monitor!

In the auditorium, all the gangways should be clear. In venues where the seating is not a fixture, it is worth checking on the regulations that govern how they should be arranged. If in doubt, talk to the local fire brigade, who will be pleased to advise. As a basic guide, gangways should be just over a metre wide and there are clear rules as to the distance between each row, although this varies depending upon the particular design of the seat.

It is obligatory to link the chairs together in lines of not less than four, and not more than twelve. In the event of a fire, this minimises the problems caused by a panic-struck audience scattering chairs every which way. Beware the occasional audience member who decides to detach a chair from the line and puts it in the gangway 'to get a better view'!

Consider in advance where you can accommodate wheelchair users. Do not embarrass them by flapping around when they arrive, deciding what to do – have a plan. For those patrons who are able to get out of their chairs and into the theatre seats, offer assistance and then remove the chair to a convenient parking place where it will not cause an obstruction. One of the team should be on hand to retrieve the chair when required. For those who need to remain in the chair for the performance, make every effort to place them where they can see and will not be in the way. Be on the alert for sticks and crutches that project into the aisle and politely ask for them to be moved out of the way.

In the event of a fire, even if it is a false alarm, all front of house staff must know what is expected of them. Even if the venue has trained permanent staff on hand, the FOH team must know where the fire exits are and where the gathering point is situated. They should be allocated a section of the audience to look after, and/or a specific exit to open. Most groups will say that it will never happen to them, but it might. One memorable performance of a local group was disrupted by a fire alarm. It turned out to have been triggered by a stray football in an adjoining room, but nevertheless, our team were put to the test and we were required to completely evacuate the building.

First aid

It is also possible that a member of the audience may require medical attention. This may be a minor abrasion or a major heart attack. Front of house should know who to contact and where to find the first aid box. Some venues will have a trained first-aider as part of the permanent staff, in others, it will be down to the company to provide one. St John's Ambulance personnel may operate in your area and be happy to provide first aid cover in exchange for two free seats. Discuss with them where they would like to sit. They normally request to be at the end of a row and usually towards the back so that they can spot a problem and deal with it swiftly. Again, do not think that it will never happen to you.

During the show

It is the responsibility of front of house to liaise with the stage manager and to give clearance so that the performance can begin. The last few minutes before the appointed time of curtain up can be hectic. Although people would not dream of being late for a professional show, audiences for amateurs are not so polite and usually arrive at the last possible moment. Obviously if there is a queue waiting for tickets, your manager will be forced to wait, but if there are uncollected tickets, but no people in evidence, then the show must go on. They may not turn up at all.

Despite late comers, the curtain should go up on time, or as near as makes no difference. Starting five or even ten minutes late is unacceptable and unprofessional. It is sensible to assign an area to members of the team for a last minute check that no audience is lurking in the bar or the toilets.

There is always someone who comes after the performance has started. A member of the front of house team should stay in the foyer for about half an hour after the curtain has gone up. As the director, you should invite your front of house manager to dress rehearsal, so that you can discuss at what point late arrivals can be shown in. This will also give him the opportunity to learn when the interval is likely to be and at what time the show will end. Latecomers cannot expect to be shown to their allocated seat, and should be quietly directed to the nearest available places, even if this means splitting the group. There will be occasions when audience cannot be admitted until after the first scene, sometimes the first act. Your manager must be polite, diplomatic, but firm.

At the end of the show it is a nice touch if he positions himself near an exit, and says a smiling 'Good night' to the departing hordes.

Protect the cast

Once 'the half' has been called, no member of cast should appear in the foyer and conversely, admiring friends and relatives should be politely discouraged from charging back stage. Messages, flowers and cards, should be sent through to the dressing room by a member of crew.

At the end of the performance, appoint a 'stage door keeper', to keep the audience away from the cast. It is disconcerting to be discovered in your underwear by a complete stranger! Cast should be asked not to leave the dressing room wearing their costume, and to have cleaned off their make-up – or at least most of it.

The unexpected

Your front of house manager should be prepared to make relevant announcements, either through a tannoy system, or by walking onto the stage. A car can have been discovered blocking a fire exit, there could be an urgent phone call for a member of the audience, one of your cast may have been delayed or taken ill. An extreme example of the unexpected happened to us at a performance of *Neville's Island*. One of the cast of four called in to say that his wife had gone into labour – two weeks early! This was early evening, and it was possible that the baby would be born in time for the actor to get to the theatre.

We kept our fingers crossed, but ten minutes before curtain up, it was quite obvious that this was not going to happen. There was no understudy and there was no other option except to cancel the performance, for the first time in our history. Our front of house manager was called upon to explain the situation to the audience, organise refunds and re-booking for the following night. All went smoothly, the vast majority booked for the next performance and there was not one cross word. The babe arrived, on cue at the moment of curtain up! The following night, we posted the details of our new 'member' in the foyer to the delight of all those 'in the know'.

ACT III

THE LAST ACT takes the characters to the end of their journey and brings the complexities of the plot to a satisfactory resolution. You have play, cast and crew – now you must harness their energies and talents to bring your vision before an audience.

Rehearsals are central to this process, but there are other threads that must be drawn together to ensure success. This section moves from early rehearsals, through the potentially traumatic experience of technical rehearsal, to the tension of the dress rehearsal and performance. It includes information about the specific challenges of competitive festivals, and, finally, some key aspects of law that you are likely to encounter along the way.

CHAPTER 14

Rehearsals

REHEARSAL IS THE time for your team to familiarise themselves with the play away from the critical eyes of an audience. It is a time for experimentation, exploration and, inevitably, mistakes. Your task is to ensure that by the week of the show, every move, line and set change is as natural as breathing. A cast and crew who are secure and confident will give a good performance.

Rehearsals should be an enjoyable experience, but never lose sight of the fact that you are there to work. From the outset, make it clear that cast should arrive on time and ready for action. As with auditions, you and your assistant should arrive a few minutes early to open the door, switch on the heating and set out the furniture.

Chatting during rehearsal must be actively discouraged. It is distracting both for you and the actors who are trying to concentrate. This is particularly true once scripts start to go down and everyone is frantically trying to remember their lines.

First meeting

Apart from the script, go along armed with paper and diary so that you can deal with any outstanding administrative matters at the start of the evening. Make a list of contact numbers, including mobile phones and e-mail addresses. This list, which should also include the technical crew, can then be circulated throughout the whole team.

Make a note of any dates, and there are bound to be a few, when someone will be missing. This is the time to discuss the play with your newly assembled cast; how you see the characters, what the set is likely to look like, what sort of costume they will wear and so on.

Then, rather than dive straight into the blocking, take the rest of the time to read through the script. This will help the cast to familiarise themselves with each other and with their embryonic characters. It will give you an opportunity to re-visit your ideas for the production, taking into consideration what the cast bring with them – both good and bad.

Start as you mean to go on, and even if you are planning an informal read-through, hold the meeting at the rehearsal venue. If the troupe gather in a private house, they will gossip more and work less!

The schedule

Don't trust to luck and take each rehearsal as it comes – you are almost certain to run out of time. Talk to any director after a first night and nine times out of ten he will say, 'If only we had had another week.' There is never as much time as you want. Take the pressure and the panic from your cast by making a detailed rehearsal schedule.

This is a daunting task for a first-timer, so here are a few tried and tested tips for planning the schedule for a three act play, assuming two rehearsals each week:

1. List the dates of each rehearsal, up to and including show week, down the left hand side of a piece of paper.
2. Write performance, technical rehearsal and dress rehearsal against the relevant dates.
3. There should be at least two full runs before show week, more if you have time.
4. The three rehearsals before that should be an opportunity to run through each act twice.
5. Now, turn your attention to the first date on your list and work out how long it will take you to block. As a rough guide, aim to block about 10-15 pages in a rehearsal of around two, to two and a half hours. Most full length plays run to 80-ish pages, so that means the basic structure should have been laid down during the first four weeks of rehearsal. Allow more time for sections that include complicated action sequences and crowd scenes. Stage fights and dance routines should be treated separately.
6. Finally, use the time that you have left for detail work on longer sections. It is worth leaving a couple of rehearsals as 'to be decided' – allowing time to re-do sections when a cast member has been absent and for tricky scenes that require extra attention.

When you have completed your outline schedule, add the dates for 'books down'. In an ideal world, the cast should arrive with lines learnt at the first rehearsal, but in the reality of amateur theatre, this is not going to happen! The sooner the actors stop clutching their books, the sooner you can start to direct, and it is not unreasonable to expect lines to be learnt once the first detail sessions have been completed. All scripts should have disappeared at least a month before show week.

This schedule is not written in letters of blood and can be changed. Sometimes you will move faster than you expected, sometimes slower, someone will be ill or called away on business. However, if you do change things around, make sure that your cast knows.

Blocking

Blocking is theatre-speak for laying down the basic moves. This is the time for deciding in what order characters come onto the stage, and from which side – not for worrying about details of intonation and expression. Think of it as creating the skeleton of the play – muscles and flesh will come later.

For these early rehearsals to run smoothly and make good use of time, it is up to the director to do some serious homework.

Set layout

Many acting editions contain a suggested set design and accompanying moves. Whilst these are undoubtedly useful, it is not essential that you follow them to the letter. For example, there are few plays that actually require a full box set, so dare to be creative.

Discuss the set with your designer and be prepared to take his advice. He is likely to know the venue and the opportunities and obstacles that it presents. For example, if the play calls for a good deal of food and cups of tea to be produced from a kitchen stage right and you only have wing space on stage left, then it would be simpler to reverse the whole thing. You cannot have a door against a wall of concrete either, so it will have to be moved. Similarly, if there is a major set change, you will need to work out where to store flats and furniture.

If at all possible, visit your stage with the designer. You may think you know the space well, but memory plays tricks and it is extremely helpful to walk the stage yourself. And a tip – look upwards. In a recent production, with a major set change, we decided to put the flats on trucks for speed and convenience. However, technical rehearsal arrived, the trucks meant that the flats were three inches taller than we had bargained for, there was a huge, immoveable projector screen hanging above the stage, and you've guessed, the flats would not fit. Technical rehearsal was abandoned while we frantically rebuilt the set!

Once the entrances and exits are located, you then need to decide where to place the furniture. This is usually straightforward and will be dictated by the play and the restrictions of the set. If you are new to directing, I would strongly advise that you avoid putting a large piece of furniture, a sofa, or a bed for example, in the centre of the stage. It can become an obstacle to movement and will make your life difficult. As with all theatre, this is a rule that can be broken when you really know what you are doing.

Preparing the script

It is obviously necessary to make notes as you plan. For rehearsals to run smoothly, these notes need to be available at a glance. Nothing is more disconcerting for a cast than a director who cannot read their own writing, or who shuffles through reams of paper trying to find the precise grouping that seemed to work so well in the comfort of his own home. It wastes time and takes away from your authority.

The vast majority of scripts do not have enough space for legible notes, so, take the script apart, break the spine, interleave each page with a sheet of plain paper and put it into a ring binder. It is then easy to record your ideas opposite the relevant section of the script. Your assistant must do the same, so that she can keep track of any changes, leaving you free to concentrate on the business in hand.

Moving the cast

You now have the key landmarks, and can begin to work out who is moving where and when. Some people have the ability to see the play in their mind's eye, others have difficulty keeping track of characters. In the latter case, it can be quite helpful to draw a rough plan of the stage and use counters, chess pieces or similar items, to represent your actors.

Blocking is the bedrock of a good performance. The time and thought that you invest at this early stage will pay dividends. Get the blocking wrong, and no matter how good the cast, the performance will lose credibility.

Blocking for work in the round, or where the audience will be seated on three sides, is not as difficult as you may think. Unlike working on a stage, the audience will be unable to see all of the action all of the time, but they will expect to see most of the action most of the time. You need to think more carefully about entrances and exits, but the key is to use diagonal positioning as much as possible. The use of diagonals will result in two sides of the audience being able to see the facial expressions of at least one actor at any one time. During the blocking process you must forgo the comfortable chair and table and walk the room, that way, you should be able to identify areas of the audience that are neglected.

Theatre depends on the suspension of disbelief and the basic foundation of maintaining the illusion of reality is to make every movement look natural. The golden rule is that each move must have motivation and purpose. If, for example, your actor is required to have a conversation while seated, and must then be elsewhere to discover a letter or look out of a window, then you must find a reason for him to make that move.

The reason can be something practical like pouring a drink. It can be driven by the character's emotional state. Anger, embarrassment and distress, are all valid reasons to move. Movement can also be used as physical punctuation, so your actor can shift his position with a change of subject, or a new thought.

No two directors will block a scene the same way. All that matters is that the final sequence must look right and feel right to the actors. Listen to your cast if they are unhappy with a move or say 'I think I should move at this point.' If they are uncomfortable, you are unlikely to get the desired effect. What seemed fine on paper, may simply not work when you get to the rehearsal, so be prepared to think on your feet and change your mind.

Don'ts

The following are best avoided by new directors. However, all these rules can be broken for specific effect.

1. Masking: do not allow one character to stand directly in front of another, particularly if the up-stage actor is speaking.

2. Up staging: do not force an actor to deliver a key speech with his face turned away from the audience. On the other hand, it is not always neces-sary to look at the person being addressed and there are occasions when speaking out front, to a character behind can be very powerful.

3. Scissors: avoid situations where two actors move across each other to opposite sides of the stage at the same time. The poor audience will not know where to look. Having said that, in plays like *Blithe Spirit* by Noel Coward, you can usefully have the 'living' actor and the 'ghost' slide past each other, to heighten the impression of invisibility.

4. Straight lines and even spacing: when three or more actors are on the stage together, they have a marked tendency to stand in a straight line, or a perfect semi circle with the same amount of distance between them. It may feel natural to them, but it will look artificial. Group them informally and stagger the spacing.

Do's

1. Hands: many amateurs have no idea to what to do with their hands. This can result in small, jerky gestures which are both meaningless and irritat-ing. Instead, encourage them to make positive gestures with the up-stage arm – using the down-stage limb will mask their face. If in doubt – keep

hands still, but do not let your gentlemen resort to plunging their hands into their pockets and leaving them there.

2. Turning: encourage your cast to turn towards the audience.

3. Diagonals: place actors at a slight angle, rather than directly opposite each other, for a more interesting and natural look.

4. Resist the temptation to keep your characters on the move. There are times when keeping still works best.

5. Back acting: to have an actor turn his back to the audience often appears in the 'don't' list. However, this move has its uses – it can isolate a character, it can pull the focus onto a silent character, and if the rest of the cast are all looking his way, it can be accusatory.

From paper to people

You have done your homework and have a clear idea of when and where the moves are likely to be. Pass this information onto the cast in bite-size chunks. These can be anything from half a dozen pages to a few lines, depending on the amount of action required. You can talk them through it before you start, move them as you go along, or use a combination of both. Encourage the cast to write these instructions on their script. It is a good idea to take along a supply of pencils, preferably with rubbers on the end!

It may seem like teaching your grandmother to suck eggs, but newcomers are not always familiar with the conventions of up stage, down stage, stage left and stage right. Up stage and down stage originate from the raked stage, so up stage is at the back, down stage is nearest the audience. Stage right and left, is taken from the actors' viewpoint as they face the auditorium.

Let them walk through the section, making any necessary changes as you go, then give them time to repeat the sequence. Running a second time will help them remember the moves, whilst giving you an opportunity to watch a more fluid version and check that it works. Keep an eye on the clock, and before the end of the rehearsal, aim to put the sections together and run through for a third time.

It is a sad fact that, unlike the professional theatre, there will be more than one rehearsal when you do not have a complete cast. There are likely to be additional dates when members will not be available that were not known at the time of auditions. If you have advance warning, then you can plan ahead, and perhaps change the date of a particular rehearsal, or alter the section of script that you work on. The unforeseen can also strike without warning. In a recent production, one member damaged her ankle and was out of action for three rehearsals. Don't panic, it is perfectly possible to work on a section with a body missing. Your assistant director can step in, either by just reading the lines, or ideally, joining the cast for that evening.

However good or bad a rehearsal has been, make a habit of giving each member of the cast something positive to take away with them. Compliments will cushion criticism, and all criticism should be constructive. Saying 'don't' is not necessarily going to help the actor improve, but, a 'why don't you try ...' can produce the desired result.

Learning lines

The primary task of an actor is to learn the script. It is impossible to direct an actor with a book permanently glued to his hand during rehearsals and if the work is not done before performance, you are more than likely going to have a show that is truly amateur, in the pejorative sense of the word. An inadequate grasp of the words results in serious stage fright, hesitation, numerous prompts and a highly embarrassed audience. I cannot stress enough how fundamental line learning is to a good performance, yet all too often, this is the area that sharply divides the professional from the amateur.

The phrase 'Take 100 lines' is associated with a punishment, and while the practice has largely disappeared from our schools, in the world of amateur theatre, lines are still regarded as something to be endured, rather than an essential tool. Everybody has a different technique for learning and some people learn faster than others. The following ideas may help your cast:

1. Tape

Hearing the script time and time again can help to impress the words on the mind. It may be that the cast come together at the start of rehearsals to record a complete reading of the play. The tape can then be copied and a cassette given to each cast member.

Actors may prefer to make a recording that is personal to them, reading aloud their own scenes and leaving a space where their dialogue should be.

Tapes can be invaluable for those who spend a good deal of their working life in a car.

2. Hide and say

Some actors take a page or two at a time and read it again and again until they have a reasonable idea of the content. They then take a card and run it down the page, read the cue, and with the lines concealed, see how much they can remember. They then remove the card, check the accuracy and repeat as often as necessary. Then they build the next speech onto the one before until happy that both pages are in the memory.

The process can be repeated with the next two pages, then all four run-together and so on. This can be done silently, but it is preferable to read out loud.

3. Using a feed

When the actor feels reasonably confident of the words, he could enlist the help of a willing ally to read cue speeches and listen to responses and prompt when necessary. The ally could be asked to tell if the words are completely scrambled, but not to stop the actor every time 'the' is said instead of 'a'. Too many interruptions and corrections are destructive rather than helpful.

4. Read and read again

As confidence increases, actors should try reading the scenes again and again. This is not as easy as it sounds, there is a tendency to say 'I know that bit' and skip to the next speech – they shouldn't. Force them to read every word, preferably aloud, so that they are both seeing and hearing the script. This technique enables actors to correct inaccurate words or phrases and should also mean that they become very familiar with the whole script.

Knowing other people's lines as well as their own will give actors the confidence to help someone out if they dry, to respond correctly to a paraphrased cue, or as can often happen, to pick up an unexpected cue when a colleague has happily jumped a few speeches.

Rehearsals are *not* the place to learn lines. Of course, if a character is not required for a scene or so, then he is more than welcome to bury his nose in his script, or go to a different area to rehearse with a colleague, but the basic, hard slog of learning must be done at home.

Be fair and realistic, by all means, but be firm. Many actors use their script as a comfort blanket, hanging on to it for reassurance, even when it is obvious they have a good knowledge of their lines. The first time a book is abandoned can be nerve-racking, but once this threshold has been crossed the actor will grow in confidence. Encourage and support them to put it down and if all else fails, physically remove it. I have known directors to take a script away and sit on it, myself included! This may sound draconian, but do it with a light touch, and they will thank you later – probably. There are times when half a scene is fine, but the actor has absolutely no idea what happens next. Don't prolong the agony and waste rehearsal time, praise them for what they have achieved and let them revert to the script.

There is a strange syndrome which every thespian is familiar with – the condition known as 'I knew it in the kitchen.' There is a stage in the learning process when you really believe you know the words in the safety of your own home, but standing in a rehearsal room is very different and your mind will go completely blank. If and when this happens to one of your cast, encouragement and good prompting will see them through.

Line runs and gabbles

Towards the end of the rehearsal process it can be helpful to put in an additional night to concentrate totally on words. This can be held in the rehearsal room or in a private house. The cast are not required to move from their seats, or worry too much about intonation, but to focus purely and simply on which line follows which.

A gabble rehearsal is an extreme version of a line run and can be usefully done during the set-up weekend. A gabble is a high speed line run, no move-ment, no intonation, no pauses, just spouting the lines as fast as they possibly can.

More challenging still, is the speed run. The cast are asked to dash through the whole play, not worrying about lines, but thinking about the sequence of the action and the key scenes.

Let's take Macbeth, the first three scenes could run something like this:-

---

Scene 1
Enter three witches.
Three witches: 'Hubble bubble'
Exit witches

Scene 2
Enter Duncan and Co.
Duncan: 'What bloody man is that?'
Captain: 'Macbeth fought really well.'
Enter Ross and Angus – Exit Ross and Angus

Scene 3
Enter three witches: 'sailor's wife' – 'pilot's thumb' – 'a drum, a drum, Macbeth doth come.'
Enter Macbeth and Banquo
Three witches: 'Hail, hail, hail.' 'Thane of Cawdor' – 'Your children shall be kings.'
Exit witches
Enter Ross: 'You're Thane of Cawdor'

> Exit Ross
> Macbeth: 'Chance may crown me' – 'let's go and meet the king.'
> Exit Macbeth and Banquo.

This is an energetic warm-up exercise, and one which is usually highly enjoyable, as cast pelt on and off, hurling lines at one another. It does have a serious purpose and will help to embed the overall structure of the play in their minds. There is also a great sense of triumph in running through a full length play in under five minutes – and getting to the end without completely corpsing!

Detail work

Once the framework has been laid down, you can begin to deal with the subtleties. Work in larger sections of around 20 pages. As a rule of thumb, a page of a standard script will run at about 2 minutes, or just under, in final performance. At this stage, there will be a good deal of stopping and starting, but you should have time to work a section and then run it, in an evening's rehearsal. Only interrupt in that final run if things are obviously going to pieces, otherwise, let your cast get the feel of how it is going to work and give notes afterwards. As the action and dialogue begins to run at a more sensible speed, it is not uncommon to find that you have blocked too many moves. Your cast may find themselves sitting down and leaping up two seconds later, or are darting frenetically around the space. Use the motivation rule to subtract the extraneous moves and offer to buy your assistant a new rubber!

The actor's job is to become someone else. He has to take a character that only exists on the printed page and turn it into a living, breathing personality that the audience can believe in. He must take the written words and speak them as if they had only just occurred to him. He must appear totally at home in a completely artificial environment. That is a pretty tall order, and he will rely on you, the director, to guide him through the mass of details that go to into the creation of a credible performance.

Detail includes everything from intonation, speed of delivery, gestures, eye contact and so on. You must therefore have your eyes and ears completely focussed on the cast. Have the script open at the right page, but watch the cast, not the written word, that is the job of your assistant. Your task is to act as a mirror for your cast and to clearly reflect back the image they create, both good and bad.

There is an enormous amount to think about and to watch for. This section skims the surface of key elements that go to make up a good production and is designed to set you thinking. This is the time to deal with any bad habits before they become an ingrained part of the performance. The most common problems are a tendency to rock from one foot to the other, flicking hair away from the face and unnecessary hand waving. All of these behaviours make an actor look insecure.

Eyes are a most expressive part of the face, and an audience is sensitive to every nuance. Eyes betray slight changes in the actor's emotional state, whether this is part of the performance or not. A nervous actor's eyes tend to have a high blink rate and flicker from place to place. This inadvertent movement is often the first warning to a prompt that an actor is struggling and could be about to dry. Even when a performer is relaxed, some may have a tendency to let their eyes wander – don't let them. Wandering eyes indicate a lack of concentration and are distracting. This problem can ruin ensemble work. It only takes one culprit in a crowd scene or a chorus to divert the audience's attention.

It is not just how you look, but the direction of the gaze which counts. When characters look out over the auditorium, supposedly watching something in the distance, it is important that they all look in the same place. This may seem obvious, but it is frequently missed and the illusion is destroyed as a result. Take time at the tech. rehearsal to pick a point for them to focus on, the exit light at the back, or a particular line of bricks.

There is also the theatrical convention of the fourth wall, the unseen barrier between cast and audience. Encourage your cast to imagine what that wall looks like – if the play is set in an interior, is there a fireplace, a television set, or a window? Help them to judge the distance of their apparent gaze accordingly. With a little practice it is possible to focus automatically on something that isn't there! You can help by standing where the wall would be to give them an idea of the distance. If the scene is set outdoors, the illusion of looking into the distance is far easier to manage. Unless you require the cast to communicate directly with the audience, strongly discourage anyone from taking a peek at the audience to see if their friends are in row B, while waiting to deliver their next line. The cast focus must be on the action on the stage at all times, and their reaction to what is happening in the world of the play.

An interesting aspect of 'looking' is mirror work. You can decide that an invisible mirror is hanging on the fourth wall, and ask an actor to check his tie. The trick is to establish the location of the glass and then look past it, to where the reflection would appear to be. Confused? Go look in a mirror and you'll see what I mean. A perfect example of intense mirror work is *Steel Magnolias*. The hair-dressing salon is often set with the chairs facing the audience, and empty frames in front of the clients where the glass would be. For this play, not only must the 'clients' work out how to look at themselves, they have to think what they might be able to see over their shoulders – through the mirror. The stylists must also remember that they would be talking to their clients in the mirror and ensure that they keep the right imaginary eyeline. Complicated, but the final effect is well worth the effort.

Many amateur actors have a bizarre inclination to stare at the 'ceiling' when they make an entrance into a room that is supposed to be new to them. No one does that in real life, so don't let them do it on the stage. The audience needs to see the faces of the actors, so if your cast have a tendency to stare at the floor, or, more commonly, to look slightly upwards giving a delightful view of their chin, tell them. Most of the time they will have no idea that this is how they behave.

Character work

A crucial part of an actor's job is to put themselves into the skin and mind of another person. Some characters leap off the page, but the majority need to be discovered during the rehearsal process. The greater the understanding that the actor has of his character's psyche, the more convincing the performance. As humans, we are adept at reading body language, facial expressions and interpreting inflexions of the voice – an audience is no different. If the character and his thought processes are clear to the actor, then it is surprising how much of this will be conveyed across the footlights. For want of a better term, I call this 'the ice-berg effect'. Two thirds of an ice-berg are hidden beneath the water, but this underlying structure is what supports the visible berg, and so it is with acting.

Help your cast by encouraging them to invent a personal biography – family background, career path, what style of clothes their character would wear, sometimes even what kind of food they like. The physical elements of a character can be enormously helpful. Many actors find their character from the shoes that they wear, which in turn affects their movement. Others construct a personality from finding a voice. A full discussion of movement and voice work would take another couple of books, so here are a few general tips that you may find helpful.

Movement

The way in which someone walks gives an instant short-cut to the character. You only have to watch people in the street for a few minutes and you find that you are making assumptions about their mood and personality. A bent figure with a walking stick in the distance is probably in their 80s, an elegant woman striding out in high heels is seen as efficient and in control, someone walking slowly, head bowed, could be depressed or thoughtful.

Rehearsals

An actor's walk often starts with the shoes they wear. Male actors get less help from shoes than their female counterparts who have a whole range of styles and heel heights to choose from. However, a man will walk very differently in wellingtons, sloppy slippers, or Cuban heel boots. Talk to the wardrobe manager and aim to get appropriate footwear for rehearsals. You can also cheat the relative height of your cast by using the right shoes – putting a tall woman into flat shoes, when she is playing opposite a shorter man can make them appear a better match.

Movement can be used to indicate age. As a general rule, the younger the character, the more flexible and fluid their movement. Middle age is a little slower and more dignified, while old age can be conveyed by slow, deliberate movements and a perhaps a slight stoop. The actor only needs to sketch these elements into their work – understatement is usually best. For example, the hunched over, quivering mannerisms that some amateurs assume makes them look ancient, are best reserved for panto or melodrama.

The speed at which an actor walks can convey mood. Agitation is represented by pacing swiftly and erratically about the stage, thought, by a measured gait. If in doubt, ask your actor to walk at a rate that matches the pace of the speech – it usually solves the problem.

Think about the way the actor sits. Posture is influenced by mood, but also by the era in which the play is set. For example, no self-respecting Victorian lady would ever dream of crossing her legs. Sitting with crossed legs is relaxed, while bolt upright, perhaps on the edge of a chair, legs firmly together, creates the illusion of tension. A young character might sit with one leg buried beneath them, or even sprawl on the floor.

The angle at which characters sit can offer clues as to their relationship with others. Experiment for yourself and put two people on a sofa:-

1. Both face forward, sit upright, legs together – they are tense and uncomfortable with each other.
2. Both face forward, sitting back, one or both have crossed legs – they are relaxed and at ease in each other's company.
3. Both sit at a slight angle, towards each other – they are interested in each other.
4. Reverse the angle so that they are turned away – they don't like each other.

Voice

If the audience are to fully understand the drama that is unfolding before them, then they must be able to hear the words. Many good productions are marred because words are rushed, swallowed or made intelligible by bad diction. Again, since voice work merits a book, not a few paragraphs, we shall aim for a few key areas.

Diction

Bad diction is inexcusable, clear diction is not difficult, but takes thought and practice to achieve. The tongue and the lips are simply muscles, and muscles should be exercised to maximise their efficiency. The easiest way to improve control over your words is tongue twisters – they are fun and they are useful. You will find a list of twisters at the back of this book.

Here is a classic exercise to get your mouth and tongue working:

Pappety	peppety	pippety	poppety	puppety
Babbedy	bebbedy	bibbedy	bobbedy	bubbedy
Tattety	tettety	tittety	tottety	tuttety
Daddedy	deddedy	diddedy	doddedy	duddedy
Kakkety	keketty	kikkety	kokkety	kukkety
Gaggedy	geggedy	giggedy	goggedy	guggedy

Breathing

Good breathing is also important to clear delivery. Many amateurs are so nervous that their breathing becomes shallow and inefficient. The end result is that their throats constrict, their vocal chords tense and they do not have enough breath to finish a sentence without it tailing into obscurity. Teach your actors to breathe deeply and slowly three or four times before making an entrance, to calm their nerves.

Most of us breathe using only the top section of our lungs. We breathe in and our shoulders move upwards slightly, but watch an opera singer and their shoulders never move. The secret is to fill the lungs, and breathing down into the little used lower section. Place one hand on your stomach and the other on your back, both at about waist height and breathe normally. You will feel a small amount of movement. Now, breathe deeply and felt the difference. You can also check your breathing by placing your hands on either side of the rib cage. Shoulders and neck should be as relaxed as possible, tension here will hinder rather than help.

Light and shade

Encourage your cast to use the full range of their voices. A line that is audible, but delivered in a monotone, is not only boring to listen to, it loses a great deal of the sense. The female voice can become shrill – suggest to your actress that she uses more breath and 'thinks' herself lower. It may sound odd, but visualising the pitch of your voice is helpful. Is it coming from your throat, chest, or stomach?

A basic level of volume is the key for audibility. Speaking at the level of normal conversation is not enough for an auditorium, so encourage your actors to give a good level of sound from the word go. Variations from this standard level add colour to a performance, but be careful of extremes. The occasional use of a quiet voice, even a whisper, is effective, use it too often and the audience will stop concentrating.

Shouting also has its place, but never confuse shouting loudly with anger. Too much shouting results in blurred diction and working at this intensity can mean that the actors find themselves with nowhere else to go. If a character is angry, experiment with a calm, deliberate delivery. The impact of furious words spoken at a lower volume can have ten times more impact than the same speech screamed to the roof tops.

Accents
Scripts can call for a specific regional accent, like *When We Are Married* by J. B. Priestley, or *Once a Catholic* by Mary O'Malley. In this case, start as you mean to go on, and ask for the requisite accent at auditions. From then on, help your cast by finding a recording of the accent that you are looking for, and give each of them a tape. The British Library have an extensive sound archive which you may find helpful.

The difficulty when one or more characters are supposed to come from the same place, is keeping them consistent with each other. If you can persuade them to keep to it, suggest that every conversation, once they step inside the rehearsal room, either in character, or out of character, is conducted in that accent. American accents turn up quite regularly and it is important that your cast all come from the same state. The accent of *Steel Magnolias* is definitely a Southern drawl, while *Death of a Salesman* by Arthur Miller will take a lighter New York style.

Adding an accent that is not specifically called for in the script can really lift a performance. Minor characters are sometimes written in two dimensions, and it can be hard to find a personality. When this happens, consider whether an accent of some description might give you a more rounded character.

Pace and cues
The last factor that helps to bring the written word to life is variety of pace and rhythm. Stressing a particular word in a sentence can completely change the sense. Take a simple line – 'I really like that'. Then say it aloud, stressing each word in turn and just listen to the different shades of meaning. When struggling with a line that does not seem to want to speak to you, as a general rule, put the emphasis on the verb.

Experiment with the pace of a speech, and if the character is walking and speaking at the same time, suggest that the actor matches the energy and speed of his gait to the speed of his delivery. Someone who is agitated and speaking rapidly is unlikely to stroll across the stage. On the other hand, someone in reflective and thoughtful mood will look odd if they dash about.

Slow cueing is responsible for marring many otherwise excellent productions. Unless there is a requirement for a deliberate pause for dramatic effect, cues must be fielded swiftly. If the next speaker is slow on the uptake, the scene will drag, or worse still, the audience will begin to think that they don't know their lines. The usual reason for the momentary pause is that the actor waits for his cue word, then breathes before speaking. Teach your cast to breathe on the last word of the previous speech and this will often eliminate the problem. Fast cueing, often in farce, or comedy, is essential and any really quick-fire sections should be rehearsed until they become reflex.

Stay in character
As rehearsals progress, actively encourage your cast to stay in character. The more adept they become at maintaining focus and characterisation, the less likely they are to be tempted to drop the façade during performance. Stepping out of character is a cardinal sin as far as the audience are concerned, at best it destroys the illusion, at worst it is embarrassing.

The cast should try to help each other out, as if they were in front of an audience. They should pick up a paraphrased cue line, not stop and tell their colleague what they were supposed to have said. Similarly, they should be able and willing to deal with a line that gets missed altogether. These errors can be dealt with at the end of the rehearsal, but learning that they can deal with unexpected problems in the safety of rehearsal will build a confidence and a trust amongst the cast that will be of massive benefit when they finally work before the paying public.

Prompts should be picked up fast without the unnecessary nicety of saying 'thank you' or the 'I was just going to say that.' Actors should focus on each other to the exclusion of anything else that might be happening in the rehearsal room. Encourage them to watch their fellow players and to listen attentively. This moment-to-moment concentration not only conveys the impression that they are seeing and hearing everything for the first time, but it will help them to stay within the reality of the play.

This level of concentration is essential for everyone on the stage, at all times. The most insignificant member of a crowd scene who stops acting and allows his attention to wander, will be immediately spotted.

Rehearsals

Corpsing

Corpsing, stage speak for smothering a fit of the giggles, is classic out-of-character behaviour. It is the theatrical equivalent of laughing at your own joke before getting to the punch line. It is self-indulgent because nine times out of ten the audience will have absolutely no idea what has provoked the outburst and they are immediately excluded. It is also dangerous, because laughter is infectious and can eat its way through the rest of the cast with disastrous results.

It is not uncommon for there to be a particular sequence of lines that two actors find impossible to get through without laughing. This is made worse if they have to look each other straight in the eyes while attempting to deliver the jinxed and often, deadly serious speech. You can help them to get over this hurdle by suggesting that they avoid direct eye-contact, and simply stare at the top of their companion's ear, thus maintaining the illusion that they are looking at each other, until the danger point has passed.

Laughter is a serious business

Many amateur companies will opt for a farce because they believe it to be easy. They could not be more wrong – good farce is harder to achieve than high drama. As with corpsing, bad farce can become self-indulgent and unfunny. Every farce is built on the premise that disaster and tragedy are around the corner – the man who slips on the banana skin could so easily have broken his neck, the characters in *The Unvarnished Truth* by Royce Ryton are facing a potential life sentence for serial killing. Farce has been defined as 'real people in unreal situations' so drill your cast to play their characters with the utmost sincerity – the more serious they are, the funnier the effect will be. Rehearse and rehearse to the point when they begin to doubt that the play was ever at all funny. Then, the week before the show, manufacture a small audience of other members of the company, who will, hopefully, laugh and give the cast that all-important belief in their work.

This invited audience can also help the actors to deal with laughter. Of course, you want the audience to laugh, but you don't want them to miss anything either. Timing a laugh is not easy. It helps to think of it as a breaking wave – the laughter builds, reaches a crescendo, and then falls away. Speak too soon, and the next line will be drowned. An actor should hear the laughter reach a climax and attempt to speak as it begins to fade.

Never, never allow your cast to play for laughs. As soon as this happens, they will have stepped out of character and the delicate fabric of the comedy will be in shreds. I once watched two young performers do a slap-stick cooking routine. The sequence as written, and as rehearsed, lasted around three minutes. However, on the night in question, one young man decided to become creative by crushing an egg on his partner's hair – the victim decided to retaliate. Both actors began to ad lib furiously, the scene went totally out of hand, and lasted eighteen toe-curling, embarrassing minutes.

Over rehearsal

Towards the end of rehearsals, you may catch comments like 'We really need an audience' or, 'We're in danger of being over rehearsed'. Personally, I do not believe that over rehearsal is possible. There is no substitute for the feeling of being so in control of the character and the text that you believe you can do anything with the role. Think of a professional company who work intensively, have a week of previews, play the same role for three months or more, and still manage to bring a freshness and a vitality to the performance. The average amateur company do less rehearsal hours, have no preview week and often only perform for three or four nights – there is really no comparison.

The stale feeling that can pervade a cast is more likely to mean that the cast have done a couple of rehearsals without finding anything new to explore and have become bored. It is your job as the director to help them find that extra new something to wake their creative juices. A shift of emphasis on a line, an additional gesture, is probably all that it will take.

Opening a show

It may seem bizarre to end this section by talking about the beginning of a play, but the first two or three minutes can influence the whole tone of the performance. An uncertain start makes both cast and audience apprehensive. Take the time to pay extra attention to the first couple of pages, until the cast are completely confident. A strong opening scene will set them up for the evening and can make all the difference between an average performance and a good one.

Games

Many amateur groups are highly resistant to any form of theatrical game. More often than not this is due to lack of confidence and a fear of looking silly, but if you can get them started, games can be beneficial and highly entertaining. Always give them advance warning, spring an exercise on an unsuspecting cast and they are unlikely to cooperate.

There are a few simple games that can be helpful in establishing character.

Hot seating

How?

Set chairs for the cast in a semi-circle, with one chair set slightly apart at the top of the arc. This is the hot seat. Each member of cast takes the metaphorical 'black chair' in turn and is interrogated by the others. The cast should remain in character throughout, whether in the hot seat or not. Questions can range from matters referred to in the script, to what they believe their background to be, do they have siblings? What is their job? Their opinion of another character?

It is important that you do your homework and have at least four or five questions for each character so that you can step in when the inspiration of the others begins to flag.

Why?

At the end of the session, the cast will have a much clearer idea of who they are than when they started. There is no limit to the power of imagination when it takes hold and the results of this exercise never cease to amaze me, whether as a participant or an observer. Actors discover that they were born of repressive parents, cannot stand carrots, have a total dislike of character X, and why they came to be in their present situation. The advantage of working this as a team, is that, again surprisingly, but with reliable regularity, the team construct a set of biographies that are interrelated and totally compatible. A secondary benefit is the number of laughs that you will have along the way!

Improvisation

How?

Ask your characters to improvise a situation, either based directly on the text, or perhaps reflecting a previous unscripted conversation that might have taken place.

Again, it is up to you to do your homework, decide what aspects of the characters it would be most helpful to explore and to come up with a suitable scenario.

The following exercise is an excellent method of building team work and trust.

Countdown

How?
Your cast, and ideally your prompt, should stand in a circle and close their eyes. The task is for someone, anyone, to say 'one', and for the process to be repeated until the group reach 20, whereupon they proceed to count back to one. If two people speak at the same time then the team must go back to the beginning and start again. Anyone can speak, at any time and, initially there will either be extremely long pauses or everyone will speak at once. There is also likely to be a fair amount of giggling. After only two or three attempts, it is amazing how quickly the cast begin to apparently read each other's minds and pick the right moment to speak.

Why?
This game helps the cast to tune into each other. It builds trust and team work and increases the actors' ability to focus on the job in hand. This is an ideal exercise to do in the dressing room about ten minutes before curtain up.

Alphabet speak

How?
Put your cast into pairs, and give each pair a specific situation. Here are a few to get you started.

1. Customer and retailer:
   The customer is returning a faulty item.

2. Learner driver and instructor:
   A driving lesson.

3. Mother and teenager:
   The mother is demanding that the child cleans their room.

4. Husband and wife:
   Who left the cap off the toothbrush?

5. A love scene.

Rehearsals

Ask the actors to improvise their scene, but they may only talk using the letters of the alphabet, preferably in sequence. The other pairs have to guess the situation.

Why?
The end results are surprisingly intelligible and illustrate the importance of stress, rhythm and pace to our understanding of a scene.

There are a number of fun variations – they must speak in the brand names of chocolate bars, using the names of animals, items of clothing etc. but be warned, the end result can be mass hysteria!

CHAPTER 15

The Final Countdown

I HAVE YET to meet anyone involved with amateur theatre who actually likes a tech. This rehearsal is vital for the smooth running of the actual performance and it can also be the most fraught. There are many things to be tried out for the first time and there are almost always time constraints.

At this point in the rehearsal process the director should step back. The tech is run by the stage manager, you are there to advise, to be consulted and to offer an opinion – which may, or may not, be acted upon. The cast must also take a back seat – this rehearsal is for the crew and is not an additional dress rehearsal. It is easy to assume that because the crew remain unseen, without lines and moves to remember, that they don't feel nervous – they do. The technical night is there to give them the same confidence and security that the cast will, hopefully, have developed during rehearsals.

The most efficient way to run a tech is cue to cue. That means starting at curtain up through to the first lighting cue, then jumping the dialogue until you come to the next cue. Only rarely is a play sufficiently simple, from a technical point of view, to allow the actors to attempt to run through the whole piece. Even then, they must be prepared to stop if there is a technical hitch.

Ideally, it should be the stage manager who prepares the list of cues. In reality, few amateur stage managers will know the play as well as the director and it will be up to you to provide him with it. Even if you know that he will come up with a list, do your own to ensure that nothing is missed. Discuss the plan for the evening with the stage manager in advance and agree who is to be responsible for what aspect. The secret of a good tech is plan, plan and plan some more.

Your list should include all sound and light cues, set and props changes, and any fast costume/make-up changes and don't forget the closing and opening of the front tabs.

Everything will take longer than you expect and will need to be repeated. Take the apparently simple task of starting a show. In practice, this opening sequence is complicated and there can be as many as 10 cues to coordinate before the first word of dialogue is spoken.

1. The stage manager calls beginners on stage.
2. Front of house manager gives clearance.
3. Working lights on stage go out.

4. House lights dim.
5. Announcement, live or recorded, about mobile phones and photography.
6. Curtain music.
7. Working lights up on stage.
8. Open tabs.
9. Lights up on stage.
10. Fade music.

Sound and lights

It is your task to finalise the volume of sound effects and music and the overall brightness of the lighting, so that these levels can then be recorded, or programmed into the equipment for the duration of the run. Pay particular attention to the volume of sound that is played under dialogue. Your aim is to enhance the actor's words, not drown them. An on-going sound effect, such as rain, wind or traffic, does not necessarily need to stay at the same volume throughout a scene. You need only to establish the effect at the beginning, then gradually fade it down during the dialogue.

Keep an eye on any dark spots that you may have missed during set up. Often, it is only when the actors are on stage that you become aware that there is a dark spot down stage left, or that the front of the apron is a touch gloomy. It is probably too late to change the position of the light, so be prepared to ask your cast to shift their positions accordingly.

Look out for any spillage of light from the wings and unexpected shadows cast by people back stage and errant torches.

If an actor is to be spot-lit and needs to hit a particular point on the stage, then this must be rehearsed. Identify the position, using either the actor or a stand-in. If you have to find the light yourself, try holding your forearm across your face, palm towards the light until you feel the heat of the lamp. It is not always possible to tape the stage, so the actor must find some form of landmark, the edge of a table or a rug, for example.

Any pyrotechnics, gun shots or similar effects *must* be tried during the tech and should have been allowed for in the budget. Smoke machines can be obstinate when faced with the actual set, and again, it may take more time than you bargained for to get the desired result. The stage manager should be given time to talk to the cast about safety procedures.

Timing cues

This is largely self-explanatory, and if your crew have managed to attend a rehearsal or two, it can be a straight-forward process. However, help them by identifying clear signals, a specific line of dialogue, or piece of business.

Sometimes you will need to resort to subterfuge to get the cue accurate. So, if there is no dialogue and a stage hand is poised to make an effect from the wings, but unable to see a thing, then the old trick of asking the actor to cough, can work really well. A classic piece of timing which often lets amateur productions down, is flicking a light switch. Solve the problem by ensuring that the actor makes a positive arm movement and ask him to let his hand linger on the switch until the light has changed. The same technique can be used when switching on a radio or a gramophone. Such cues may need to be repeated two or three times until both actor and operator are confident.

At the end of a scene, rehearse the sequence – lights on stage down, music up, tabs close (if used), working lights on, and reverse the process at the start of the next.

Set and set changes

Cast a critical eye over the set, which should be complete, or at least, almost complete. Check that the joins between flats are concealed and that there are no areas of unpainted wood on door frames and such like. Ask the cast to make a point of testing doors and handles and make sure that they neither stick shut or fail to open! They also need to be aware of which way a door will open! Traditionally, a door should open onto the stage, but this is yet another theatrical rule that may have to be broken.

Check the sight lines with the stage manager so that he can tape the wings. Now is also your last chance to suggest that a pot plant might cover that empty corner, or to ask for a picture on the wall. Setting and striking of props should be fast and accurate. Never leave an audience in the dark for any longer than you have to – 30 seconds is about as much as they can cope with before they become restless. The use of appropriate music always helps to cover the pause in the action without breaking the mood. Even the simplest change should be rehearsed and those that require two or more crew to get everything done should be carefully choreographed. The aim is to have all props in their correct place in the fastest possible time and with the minimum noise. The last thing you want is for crew members to crash into each other in the gloom, have two people trying to move the same chair, or worse still, start the next scene with an item in completely the wrong place because everyone assumed that someone else had moved it.

Ideally, this basic routine will have been worked out at rehearsal by the props mistress and her team and the tech provides an opportunity for fine tuning. If, however, you discover that the groundwork has not been done, then you may need to step in. Scene changes that are done without closing the tabs need to be super-slick and professional, as, despite the dim light, the audience will be watching. If the set allows, use more than one entrance, this speeds up the process and minimises the risk of the crew getting in each others way. Remember to retain the credibility of the set and don't allow props to enter from a balcony window that is supposed to be ten feet up. The audience may not totally realise why this looks wrong, but it will strike an odd note.

The crew should look professional. Standard back-stage clothing is known as blacks, and black they should be, right down to the shoes – a flash of gleaming white trainers can be very distracting! Ladies of the team are well advised to wear trousers and everybody should have quiet soles. If the script gives you the opportunity to put the crew into costume making them an integral part of the show, then do so.

Major set changes that require flats and furniture to be shifted can take considerable time to practise, whether you have the luxury of the main interval, or only a minute or two. The stage manager will need to organise for the props to be cleared and placed out of harm's way. He must then choreograph his team to strike and set the scenery before the new props can be put in place. Unless you are absolutely desperate for time, this type of change should be practised at least twice.

No matter how well you plan, the unexpected can always happen – the important thing is to stay totally calm! In an earlier section I explained how we misjudged the height of the flats once they had been put onto trucks, and as a result, the technical rehearsal was abandoned after the first act while we rethought and rebuilt the set. We survived the experience without a cross word, finished the tech during dress rehearsal, and ended up with a good show.

Costumes and make-up

Quick changes of costume and make-up should be built in to the evening's schedule. The changes will have been rehearsed, but there is a big difference between working in a brightly lit rehearsal room with no time pressure and struggling in the gloom and haste of back stage. When an actor needs to change in the wings in the interest of speed, the changing area should be agreed with the stage manager. It is important that this does not obstruct the crew, and equally important, that the crew do not obstruct the change.

Costume and make up are not essential elements of the tech, and although it can be helpful to see the overall effect, they can be sacrificed if it means you can save time. Naturally, if there is any suspicion of wet paint, costumes should be positively forbidden!

Even if time is fast running out, talk to the stage manager and lighting about the curtain call. If necessary, run through the sequence without the actors, and rehearse them at the dress. It will speed up the process if the bows are taken in time with lights, rather than opening and closing the tabs. As with the opening moments of a show, there are more cues than you might think. The sequence after the closing line will go something like this:

1.   Closing music (if any)
2.   Lights down
3.   Tabs shut (if any)
4.   Stage lights on
5.   Tabs open
6.   Final lighting state
7.   First bow
8.   Lights down and straight up
9.   Second bow
10. Lights down and up
11. Final bow
12. Lights down
13. Tabs close
14. House lights up

Dress rehearsal

This is the night that the team must sink or swim – without you. The only role that you have is to give a few notes at the end of the evening. And I do mean a few. It is far too late to make radical suggestions, the cast will only become confused and uncertain. Any comments that you make at this stage should be designed for the greatest improvement with the minimum change. Be selective, and don't pick up on every tiny flaw, a move that is not precisely as planned, but looks fine should be left alone. This sort of detail will sort itself out in performance. Above all, be encouraging and constructive.

Your team should aim to do the best performance that they possibly can – a good dress is the precursor of a good performance. The old saying 'Bad dress rehearsal, good performance' is too often used to make everyone feel better if things have gone badly wrong, and is simply not true. If the show is not in good shape at the dress, then it is unlikely to rise to great heights during the run. That said, sometimes a good cast become complacent and a truly appalling dress rehearsal can frighten them back into concentration and focus.

Curtain call

Organising the final line up for the curtain call is usually rehearsed at the last minute due to time pressure. Nevertheless, it must be rehearsed at some point, or you risk a mad and unprofessional scramble. Sometimes a curtain call is rehearsed ten minutes before the curtain goes up on opening night! Since you can find yourself having to direct the call at high speed, it is important to have planned it out in advance.

As the lights go down on the final line, the cast should be ready and waiting in the wings. Speed is of the essence, the play is over, and however much the audience have enjoyed it – they want to go home! For a large cast, use every available entrance, and throw credibility to the winds. There may be only one 'door' on the set, but there will be other routes onto the stage – use them. For an ensemble piece it is nice to go for a line up of the whole cast, with the leads in the centre. Other calls may work better if the company enters in appropriate pairs, starting with the smallest roles and moving through to the main players.

However you choose to arrange the final line-up, there will be a company bow. All the company should bend slowly from the waist, and back up again. And they should do it at the same time! Identify an actor, at the centre of the front line, and ask the rest of the cast to take their lead from him. If you are reading this, thinking 'of course my cast know how to take a bow', I have to say, that a surprising number don't and a ragged curtain call takes the edge off a show. Three bows is enough, always leave the audience wanting more. If the house is half empty, the applause may only run to two, so brief your cast and lighting technician accordingly.

Finally, the practice of presenting bouquets on stage at the end of the final curtain call should be completely banned. Flowers, and even worse, speeches, are of no interest to the audience and should be restricted to the dressing room or the after show party.

Show time

Tonight, you are really out of a job, and you should also be out of the way! The cast will appreciate a good luck card and a swift visit to the dressing room half an hour before the performance. However, they will not appreciate a director who flaps and fusses, and tries to give notes in that last precious half hour, or heaven forbid, one who dives in during the interval with last minute change or two. It is too late. Accept that there is nothing you can do, provide yourself with a glass of wine, keep your fingers crossed and remember to breathe!

Watching your cast perform can be a far worse experience than stage fright – at least stage fright fades once you step on the stage, and at least if you are on stage when things go wrong there is perhaps something you can do to help. There is no such respite for a director, who must sit and sweat all the way through. Do try and steel yourself to watch. Some directors find the whole thing so traumatic that they hide in the bar and never see the fruits of their labours. Your cast and crew look to you for praise and reassurance and they will be disappointed if you have not seen their triumphs or disasters.

Find yourself a seat in the body of the auditorium, don't intensify their nerves by smiling up at them from the front row! In the interval and at the end of the performance it can be rewarding to listen to passing comments, but don't go fishing for compliments.

Audiences are like people – all different. Some laugh or cry at the drop of a hat, others sit there waiting for you to entertain them. If the audience is unresponsive, then it is up to the cast to work harder to engage their interest. Don't fall into the trap of blaming the audience for a poorly received performance – 98% of the time it is not their fault!

CHAPTER 16

Drama Festivals

ENTERING THE WORLD of competitive festivals is not for the faint-hearted. Your skills as a director will be tested to the limit and so will your nerves. It is not easy to perform in a new venue without a full technical rehearsal and certainly, with no dress rehearsal. A festival will stretch the ingenuity and skill of your crew, who must devise a portable set, erect and strike within the prescribed time limit and work with unfamiliar equipment. The pressure on the cast is enormous and they must be supremely confident of their lines and moves, otherwise nerves can get the better of them. As if that was not enough, you will then have to listen to the adjudication, which may praise or criticise all your hard work. That said, festivals are intended as a celebration of theatre and should not only be enjoyable, but an opportunity to learn and improve your art. Win or lose, a company can reap enormous benefit by entering.

There is no substitute for hands-on experience, and I strongly recommend that you should have attended a number of festivals and competed in a least one, prior to taking on the role of director.

Rules and regulations

Before going anywhere near a play catalogue, get hold of a copy of the rules of the festival and the syllabus. They vary slightly across the areas, so do not assume that what is required by one will be acceptable to another. The rules and the syllabus will tell you the categories that are available, the time limits and the number of cast and crew that you can use.

Most festivals have a section for youth teams, an all-women entry, an open category and sometimes, a section for short plays, usually under 20 minutes. It is worth casting your eye over the trophy list as well. There may be an opportunity to go for best set, best original play, or best ensemble work.

Some local festivals offer the opportunity to enter the *All England Theatre Festival*. This is a nationwide competition of one act plays. A team can progress through to the English final and ultimately compete against teams from Scotland, Ireland and Wales.

The All England rules demand that an entry should be a minimum of 20 minutes and must not exceed 55 minutes. This includes any set changes within the performance. There are severe penalties for poor time-keeping, either under or over. For example, up to 1 minute over or under, you will lose 1 mark, not too serious, but 4 minutes out of line and you will lose 10 marks.

The chosen play must have a minimum of two speaking parts on stage, though there are some festivals which will allow monologues. It is possible to choose an extract from a longer play, but only if the excerpt is understandable to a member of the audience who is unfamiliar with the whole piece. For example, my company entered Act 1 and Act 3 of *Steel Magnolias* by Robert Harling. The removal of the second act does not detract from the basic story of the play. (Be warned – it ran exceptionally close to the wire in terms of time.)

If you take this route, you must, must, must, get full permission from the relevant agents before you submit your entry and certainly before you start rehearsals. You will be asked to provide evidence of this permission by the festival organiser. As a general rule, plays that need to be cut in this way are best avoided, particularly by the inexperienced.

A small point, but one which can take companies new to festival work by surprise, is that curtain calls are not permitted.

Back stage does not escape the rule book either. The number of crew may be restricted, depending on the size of the venue. Each team is allowed a maximum of 10 minutes to set-up and five minutes to strike. No team may use recorded speech, film projection or television material without the express permission of the responsible committee. Similarly, the festival committee should be notified of any unusual effects, naked lights, pistol shots etc. and their decision is final.

This is just a taste of the rules, there are more, so always make sure you are completely familiar with your chosen festival's rules. The organising committee, particularly those involved in the All England Theatre Festival, take them very seriously and a breach can lead to disqualification.

Choose the play

First, as with all productions, you, the director, must be excited by the script. Second, your pool of actors and technicians may be more limited than for a mainstream play because of availability problems. The precise date of performance is rarely available at the time of casting – you will know the week, but not the day. Likewise, the time slot for stage viewing will also be an unknown. Finally, if you are intending to enter the AETF, remember, you could win! The dates of the subsequent rounds should be known at auditions and your cast, and your crew, need to guarantee that they will continue to be available. This undertaking is one of the few that must be written in letters of blood. Festivals have had many problems in the past with groups who have withdrawn. These days, once your entry has been accepted, you are considered to have entered into a formal contract to give a public performance. The show *must* go on, even if a principle part has to be read.

Assuming you have enough bodies available, go ahead and find a well-written script. The quality of the play will not be under scrutiny, unless of course, there is a Best Original Play section, but good material will give you a head start.

Money

A festival entry costs money. There are the standard costs as for any production, royalties, costume hire, and scenery, plus an entry fee, but there is no income. Your company may be able to afford this outlay, but some groups will be deterred by the expense. There are ways to recoup some of the money. The company can choose to take an act from an existing mainstream production, but be wary of extracts as was said earlier. There is also the possibility of turning the festival entry into an event in itself. It is sometimes possible to link with another local group and perform both offerings as an evening's entertainment, perhaps with a simple supper in the interval, sharing costs and proceeds. If there is no companion group, you could add a series of sketches or readings to flesh out the evening.

Festivals have financial issues of their own and while a separate performance of your entry will help your group, it will potentially take away from festival audience. The festival movement are fighting to keep this invaluable area of amateur theatre alive, so please bear this in mind. Some festivals are addressing the problem by offering a certain number of tickets to participating groups at a discounted rate, which you can then sell on at a small profit.

Interpretation and style

Consider whether the play you have selected will lend itself to a slightly unorthodox interpretation. It is important that the play is presented in line with the author's original intention, but within that restriction, it may be possible to sprinkle a little extra theatrical magic that will make your production stand out from the crowd. Think about the themes of the script and ask the following questions:

- Can you use a stylised set rather than a realistic one?
- Will it benefit from music?
- How creative can you be with lighting?
- Could carefully chosen colours help?
- Would a particular style of costume help?

Whatever style you choose, it is vital to be consistent throughout. The key to good festival work is serious attention to the tiny details which should come together to form a coherent whole. A prop out of period, a pair of shoes that do not look right, can lose you vital marks.

Set design

Designing a festival set is a real challenge. It must serve the play, be adaptable for different venues, be fast and easy to erect and above all, it must be portable. The cost of van hire can make a major dent in the budget, so it is worth designing a set that can be transported by an estate car, or two, and a roof rack. Traditional box sets are out of the question, indeed, they are explicitly forbidden by festival rules. However, the limitations imposed on a festival team are often beneficial and lead to inventive and interesting sets. Never underestimate the magic of imagination that can transform everyday items into something else entirely. *Soapsud Island* by Phillip Sheahan deals with the lives of laundry girls, moving from the wash house to the seaside, a fairground and a charabanc. The only set required is six large laundry baskets which are transformed into a big wheel, a coach, a row of deck chairs. Similarly, benches can become pillars, a school room, or a piano.

Stage viewing

Sometime before festival week, your team will be offered the opportunity to visit the venue and sort out the technical aspects of the production. This time is limited and strictly controlled by the festival to ensure that each team has the same opportunity. Do not waste it. It is not an extra rehearsal, but the only chance you have to set lighting levels, sound levels, and organise cues.

Prior to the viewing you will have been sent a plan of the stage, the lighting rig and, hopefully, the specifications of the sound equipment i.e. CD, mini disc or tape. Make sure that your technicians are given copies as soon as possible and if there are any areas of uncertainty, always, always check. It is also vital that sound, lights and stage manager attend two or three full runs of the play. The more familiar they are the better, since they have a great deal to do in a very short space of time.

Festivals are hard on the nerves at the best of times, and working in a totally alien setting is not recommended. Members of the team unfamiliar with the theatre should be encouraged to use the viewing afternoon to find out where the dressing rooms are, how to get to the stage, and gain a general picture of the space they will be working in.

Your core crew should go along to the viewing armed with a fully marked-up script and any necessary equipment. This may seem obvious, but it is very easy to leave something crucial, like all the sound effects, behind.

The main task of sound is to set the levels of music and effects. If you are using music under dialogue, don't guess. Run the relevant section with the actors since acoustics vary enormously. Should you require the sound to come from behind the actors, it is more than likely that you will need to bring your own equipment. Most places have speakers in the auditorium, but stage speakers are less common.

Lights have to work with the festival technician to plot the cue sequence. Again, special requirements, such as a spot on a particular stage area, should have been discussed with the festival in advance to discover if this is feasible, or if it is permissible to bring extra kit. Bear in mind that one lighting rig can be covering over a dozen plays and it is not possible to please all of the directors all of the time, so you may have to compromise.

As director, stand yourself in the centre of the auditorium to listen and watch. Ideally, try to run each cue, from the opening of the curtains to the final fade, in sequence, but be prepared to multi-task!

First impressions count. A fully prepared team that makes swift decisions and gives clear instructions will get the festival crew on their side. Bad tempered and vague teams can alienate the very people that they must ultimately rely on.

The cast can use the time to walk the stage, try out moves and so on, while you deal with the technical side. Encourage them to run a few lines of dialogue to test the acoustics. Naturally the sound waves will be different with an audience in place, but every little helps!

If you have not already done so, this is a good time to remind the cast that there is no curtain call after a festival performance.

Props and stage management can check where scenery is to be stored and will be expected to work under the instruction of the resident stage manager. You are not on home ground and every company has its own methods of running a show. It is important that your crew and the festival technicians speak the same language.

Publicity

Sadly, not all festivals are well attended and teams can find themselves playing to only a handful of audience. Performing with little or no feedback is like acting in a vacuum and not the ideal atmosphere to extract the best from the actors. For the most part, festivals rely on societies to bring supporters, so do your best to make this happen. As soon as the date of your performance is known, publicise the details to your members and encourage them to go on more than one night to check out the opposition! Rehearsals permitting, your team will benefit from making the effort to go along on another night. There is a good deal to be learnt from watching other people and listening to the subsequent adjudication.

On the last night of festival week, it is important that your company is represented. Not only does it show support for the event, but you may actually win something and it is embarrassing to announce an award and have no-one to claim it. A handful of festivals have introduced the idea of a recall night. On the last night, two plays are selected by the adjudicator to do a second performance. The plays are chosen for their entertainment value and are not necessarily the winners. This evening is purely for enjoyment, there is no adjudication and the shows are usually followed by the presentation of awards. This non-competitive evening restores the celebratory element to what can otherwise be a stressful experience.

On the night

As with all productions, the director is redundant. Your job is to wish your team well, trust them, and keep out of the way!

The adjudicator

The final verdict on your efforts will rest on one person and one person only – the adjudicator. This can be comforting if you do not agree with his decisions – it is only one person's opinion. However, always listen to the comments and suggestions with an open mind – you may learn something. After all, one of the aims of festival is to send teams away with a greater understanding of their craft. It is also worth remembering that GODA adjudicators are carefully selected and will all have undergone a rigorous selection procedure. They are not allowed to rest on their laurels and are continually monitored by the Guild and the festival committees.

What does he do?

An adjudicator will have had the scripts in advance and will have read them thoroughly. At the end of the evening his comments should cover all aspects of the production, and his criticism should be constructive and useful to the teams. The means of deciding who takes home the silver is a carefully thought-out marking scheme.

There are no second chances in festival and an adjudicator can only comment on the performance that he has seen. Live theatre is a fragile creature and things can, and do, go wrong. Occasionally the fault is completely outside your control, a bulb may blow and ruin that special effect, a sound desk can develop a fault. If this happens to you, don't panic. Discuss the problem with the festival organiser and ask for the adjudicator to be informed. Likewise, if one of your cast is unfortunate enough to have to perform with a migraine, or broke a limb the day before, by all means let the adjudicator know, but never, never beset him with a list of minor excuses.

Marking

Your entry will be marked by the adjudicator out of a possible 100. 75 marks and over is seen as very good, 60–74 is good, 40–59 is fair, score under 40 and you have a problem!

The marks are usually apportioned in the following way:

Stage presentation	15
Production	35
Acting	40
Endeavour, originality and general attainment	10

Stage presentation
This section covers the set, properties, costume and make-up, sound and lights. It may seem few marks for a good deal of work, but there is a serious reason behind this allocation. It prevents a well-off group gaining undeserved marks because it can afford to hire expensive props and scenery.

Production
This section includes the physical moves and the grouping. It will cover the pacing of the piece and whether theatrical points have been made effectively. An important question in the section is whether you have reflected the meaning of the play and have successfully interpreted the author's intention. No matter how good your direction, if you have failed in this, then marks will be deducted.

Acting
This is more straightforward. Your cast will be marked on their performance, characterisation, movement, vocal ability and so on. The adjudicator will be looking for the overall effect, one brilliant performance in an otherwise poor cast will not save the day. Solid and consistent performances from the whole team is the way to go.

Endeavour

This section is sometimes referred to as 'dramatic achievement' and gives the adjudicator the opportunity to reflect his impression of the performance as a whole. For example, a company can be rewarded for originality and effort, or for choosing a particularly challenging play.

The verdict

It is hard to listen to criticism objectively, however constructive, but do your best. The vast majority of adjudicators give careful thought to their comments and there will probably be an opportunity for you to discuss the finer points with him at the end of the evening. It is also likely that, for a fee, your company can request a written adjudication that can be considered at leisure.

If you have a second opportunity to perform your play, take the adjudication on board, but resist the urge to change things in a hurry or against your better judgement. I have seen teams make drastic changes to a production because of one adjudication, only to have the next adjudicator suggest they might think about doing what they did in the first place.

Think before you change – will the alteration clash with the overall concept of the play? Will the actors become confused if there is a massive blocking change? Does it work for you? Thinking comments through carefully and objectively – that word again – before reaching a decision will hone your directorial skills.

Of course, it is terrific to be a winner, but there should be no losers at a drama festival. Any team that has endured, and hopefully, enjoyed, this testing experience deserves to be congratulated.

CHAPTER 17

Law and the Theatre

THE MAKE-BELIEVE world of theatre does not escape from the law of the land and amateurs are no exception. The following chapter includes some of the legislation that affects your production, but is by no means exhaustive, so be careful.

Copyright and wrongs

It is important to understand that copyright laws exist to protect the integrity of the author's work and to ensure that those who have sweated blood over their writing are financially rewarded for their skill.

Once you have decided upon a play, check that the performing rights are available and how much they will cost. A published script that is in copyright will carry details of who to contact, and if you are in any doubt, consult the publisher. The cost varies – one act plays attract a lower rate than full length and musicals can be very expensive. Never embark upon a production without written permission. There are times when a script is available, but the amateur rights are not. This is usually because a professional company are touring the piece, or planning to do so. And no, means no. It is no use thinking that your audience is too small to make any impact and going ahead regardless – you run a real risk of being found out and closed down. Permission must also be obtained for a public reading of a script, no matter that it is not a full blown performance with all the trimmings.

Private or domestic performances can escape the charge, as can some performances in institutions, but never assume, always check. In some cases it is possible to apply for a free licence.

Some groups have the mistaken belief that performances for charity are exempt. This is not the case. It is possible that the owners of the copyright will be sympathetic and either reduce the fee or waive it entirely, but you must ask.

Copyright means exactly what it says. You must apply for the right to make a copy of the work in any form. You cannot get round the rules by typing your own version – it is still a copy. Some societies photocopy scripts to save money – don't. In the first place it is illegal, and anyway, the cost of copying will probably be almost as much as if you bought the real thing. That said, if a play is out of print, the publisher will almost always give you written permission to make photocopies, but is likely to make a charge for this right.

Plays cease to be in copyright at the end of the 70th year following the death of the writer. Be careful though, it used to expire 50 years after the playwright's death and because this change is relatively recent, some authors were brought back into the copyright fold. Never assume, always check.

Videos

Videos are another no-go area. There is an urban myth that it is fine to make a video for training purposes, or for the archive, and it is, indeed, a myth. If you wish to make such a recording, you must seek permission and there are occasions when permission is granted.

Cuts

Once you have the performing rights safely bought and paid for, do not fall into the trap of thinking that you are now free to take liberties with the script and cut out great chunks – you are not. Publishers and copyright owners are not unsympathetic, so it is worth seeking permission. This situation usually arises when a company wishes to enter an extract, or adapt a play to meet festival time limits. The organisers of the festival will insist on seeing the agreement. Should you choose to do two acts from a three act play, there is usually a requirement that the two acts are clearly separated, either by a black out, or by lowering the curtain.

Music

The music that you use also comes with rules and regulations attached. Music in dramatic presentations is controlled by the Performing Rights Society. A dramatic presentation is defined as a theatre production, a concert, or an event that portrays a story using either one, or all of the following elements: costume, scenery, narrative and dramatic action.

Any performance of copyright music, live or recorded, that takes place outside the home is regarded as a public performance and will usually require a licence. Licences are issued to the owner of the premises where the music is to be performed and the fee is often based on the capacity of the venue. The licence covers incidental music i.e. music that is not supposed to be heard by the cast, so you can use music to cover set changes and to underscore dialogue with a clear conscience. However, once the melody enters the world on stage, for example, if the actors are supposed to hear an orchestra playing in the distance, or listen to the radios, or whistle a tune, it enters the class of interpolated music. This is not covered by the standard licence and you should seek advice. So, if you play the theatrical game of using a piece for a set change and shifting the sound to say, a radio on the stage as the lights go up, be careful. Once the music has moved into the action it is no longer licensed, despite the fact that it is the same track. This form of music is still under the umbrella of the Performing Rights Society, but specific permission is required from them for each production. In some cases, they may refer you to the publishers of the work concerned, and although there is no guarantee that a work will be available, problems are rarely insurmountable.

The rules are further complicated because there are two forms of rights attached to dramatic presentation. 'Small rights', controlled by the PRS, apply to music that has not been specially composed for the play. 'Grand rights' apply when the music has been written specifically for a production, and with very few exceptions, are not under PRS control. The majority of scripts which include specific music will have details of where to obtain the necessary permissions, but if you are in any doubt, check with the publisher. Interestingly, pantomime is an exception and is automatically licensed.

As with all legal and copyright matters, if in doubt, ask the experts. You will find that they will do their best to help and advise. This section may seem draconian, but this is one of the few times when amateur theatre comes up against the law of the land, and it is also the area where rules are most often flouted. Short-cuts can land a company in trouble, so take it seriously.

Children

There has been an enormous amount of publicity in recent times concerning the safety of children and the checking of criminal records. Under the Protection of Children Act 1999 it is not mandatory for amateur groups to run a criminal record check on members who are working with children under 18, although some local authorities are making it a condition of licence. It is considered good practice for a society to have a Child Protection Policy and any group that wishes to apply for charitable status is now obliged to submit such a policy to the Charity Commission with their application.

Whatever the circumstances, your society must take responsibility for the chaperoning and welfare of any young person involved with a production and it is in everybody's interest to develop a policy that minimises the risks.

It is sensible to provide a chaperone who is well-known to the group rather than a newcomer, and wherever possible, a second adult should be present. If you have to use someone who is not previously known to you, make it very clear from the beginning that a Disclosure may be required and that a conviction is not necessarily going to prevent them taking the position. You should ask for proof of identity, at least one reference from someone who has experience of the applicant's work with children and details of any previous convictions. If you have any doubts, or are required to do so by the local authority, you should go ahead and obtain a Disclosure. This process can take several weeks, and is not something that should be left to the last minute.

A Disclosure is a document containing information held by the police and government departments that is provided by the Criminal Records Bureau. It is worth noting that it is usually the individual who applies for the Disclosure, not the society. The information is obviously sensitive and must be stored and handled carefully so that it is not open to abuse. The process is covered by a code of practice which can be obtained from the CRB by calling 0870 90 90 811 or from the website on www.disclosure.gov.uk. The website gives clear guidelines and is worth a visit.

NODA is registered with the CRB as an umbrella body and has the power to counter-sign applications on behalf of its members. For current details of the policy and procedure you should contact them direct. The organisation can also supply members with a model Child Protection Policy.

The CRB only covers England and Wales, so societies in Scotland should contact the Central Registered Body in Scotland on 01786 849777. Arrangements for Northern Ireland have not yet been announced.

It is more than likely that the law surrounding this delicate issue will change during the life of this handbook, so always check that your information is up to date.

CHAPTER 18

Superstitions

THEATRE IS AN uncertain business, and unlike cinema, there are no retakes when lines are fluffed, or a handle comes off in your hand – what happens, happens. Every performance, professional or amateur, is an adventure. It is hardly surprising, therefore, that a wealth of superstition and ritual has developed. Interestingly, many of these beliefs seem to be founded either on good practice or have a strong bias in favour of saving money.

The Scottish Play

Every actor is aware that the dreaded word 'Macbeth' is an anathema and should never pass the lips of anyone in the theatre, else some disaster will not be far behind.

There are various methods for deflecting the spell, the ones that I know seem to involve the culprit leaving the scene of their crime and turning round three times before they are allowed to return. A symbolic unwinding of the charm, perhaps. Sometimes the individual is also required to spit, or pass wind – no wonder they are sent outside! A more subtle means of removing the curse is to quote Hamlet: 'Angels and ministers of grace defend us', (Act 1 scene 4).

The origins of this belief vary. In Shakespeare's day, it is possible that the incantations of the witches were believed to be based on actual spells that would conjure up evil spirits. A second, more logical theory, is that since much of the action of the piece takes place in dim lighting, it is easy for accidents to happen. Apart from the dim light, the play calls for fighting with heavy, and therefore dangerous, broadswords. On top of these hazards there are a number of special effects, which as we all know, have a habit of refusing to work on the night! However, the explanation that I prefer has a mercenary flavour. In the days of stock companies, the team depended on their audience for income – not that this sounds foreign to amateur companies these days. When takings were low, the company would frantically look about for a crowd-pleaser, and what better than *Macbeth* – passion, ghosts, blood and a good plot. Hence, if this play was even being discussed, it meant that the company was in serious financial trouble.

Break a leg

A well meaning 'Good Luck' before a performance, can make an actor shudder. The phrase 'Break a leg' is a much more acceptable thing to say. Again, the origins of this are unclear.

It is said that the phrase has its origins with the assassination of Abraham Lincoln while at the theatre in 1865. The president was shot by the actor, John Wilkes Booth, who then leapt from a balcony onto the stage, breaking his leg in the process. He still managed to travel some distance before being finally caught. This is a touch obscure, perhaps in some way it represents a triumph over adversity, but Booth was still caught. Interestingly, there is the legend that Lincoln was reading 'The Scottish Play' the night before his death.

The logical explanation has roots with medieval archers when 'to break a leg' meant to bend one knee before firing. Maybe 'breaking a leg' can be said to mean 'Go out there and knock 'em dead.' Even more credible, is that the movement resembles a curtain call bow, so the phrase takes on the feel of 'be wonderful and enjoy the applause.'

Whistling

Like saying the 'M' word, someone who whistles in the theatre risks serious disapproval. The explanation for this superstition is straightforward. In the days before pagers and intercoms, the stage crew were cued by a code of whistles, similar to that used on board a ship. The sound of a whistle could therefore trigger the crew to fly scenery in or out at completely the wrong time – bad for the play and dangerous for any actor standing in the wrong place. The generic term 'crew', used for the backstage team, is likely to have a naval basis. After all, like a sailing ship, old theatres relied on athletic scrambling high above the stage and a complex system of ropes and pulleys. If this is the case, then the term 'to rig' makes complete sense.

Green

It is said to be unlucky to wear a green costume. In the time of morality plays, green was often used to represent the devil in disguise. It is also a notoriously difficult colour to light, even today, and in the time of limelight, the colour would be washed out by the green-tinged flares.

Green has strong associations with the theatre. 'The Green Room' is still used to mean a place where actors can retreat from the stage and relax – either dressing room or the bar. In the 16th century, it was common practice for a green baize cloth to be laid on the stage prior to a death scene, so that when the actor expired his costume would remain clean. The cloth was stored in the dressing room, hence the name. Perhaps another reason for not having a green costume was that it could be laid on the baize by mistake, and be lost as a result of the camouflage!

Bad dress – good performance

This expression is frequently used to give a team reassurance after a disastrous dress rehearsal. The belief does have a perverse logic, for if a team do really well at the final run through, they can become over-confident and lose the edge of concentration that fear and adrenaline provide, resulting in a pedestrian first night.

The last line

Another common superstition is that you should never, never, speak the final line of the play until the first performance. I have been told this is because the play is unfinished without the presence of an audience and should remain so until the combination is complete. I remain unconvinced. Personally, I would rather rehearse the last line so that the stage manager knows the final cue!

Flowers

Fresh flowers on stage are said to bring bad luck, but this belief has to be down to money. Flowers wilt and die under hot lighting and are expensive to replace.

Cats

A cat in the theatre is said to be lucky – presumably because they keep down the mice that would otherwise nibble at expensive props and costumes. On the other hand, a cat that crosses the stage is unlucky. A cat on stage during performance would be disruptive to say the least. Kicking a cat is also bad news, not only for the cat! Any actor lifting a foot to an invading feline would be more than likely to lose his balance, his lines, or both.

Keep the light on

A lesser known tradition is to leave a single light burning between perform-ances. It was said that a theatre without light would attract a ghost. Certainly the dense blackness of an auditorium and stage, littered with sharp props and booby-trapped with chairs, would attract an accident if nothing else. Even today, when a theatre closes, we say that it has 'gone dark'.

Epilogue

SO, YOU HAVE reached the end of this whistle-stop tour of the world of directing amateur theatre. Despite the mountains of jargon, the technical mysteries and a whole collection of rules and regulations, never forget that we put ourselves through this demanding process for the sheer love of it. There is nothing to match the pleasure that you feel at the end of a successful production, though I have yet to meet a director who is ever completely satisfied with the end result! There is always more to learn, always something that you can do better, but once bitten by the directing bug, you will find yourself being drawn to the next script like a moth to a flame!

Break a leg!

Theatre Speak – A Glossary

Apron	the section of the stage that projects into the audience
Bar/barrel	scaffolding that supports the lanterns
Barndoors	shutters fitted to fresnel lanterns to shape the light
Blacks	heavy black curtains
Blocking	planning the moves for the actors
Boards	the stage – as in 'to tread the boards'
Box set	a set made from flats occupying three sides of the stage
Braces	adjustable supports for flats
Cans	headphones
Corpse	to giggle inappropriately – and out of character
Crossfade	a change in lighting state where some lanterns increase in brightness at the same time as others decrease. Can also be used in reference to sound
CYC	short for cyclorama – plain cloth at the back of the stage
DBO	short for 'dead black out'
Dimmer	controls the brightness of lanterns
Down stage	the area of the stage nearest the audience
Drapes	curtains
Dress	short for dress rehearsal – the final run before opening night
Dry	to forget the lines
Flats	the panels that make up the scenery, either wood or canvas
Flies	the area above the stage
Flying	to drop scenery onto the stage from above
Focus	to adjust the size of a beam of light
Front of house	the area occupied by the audience – usually the foyer
Gaffer	magic heavy duty tape, beloved of techies, that can fix anything!
Gel	flame retardant cellophane that changes the colour of lights

Directing Amateur Theatre

Gobo	a perforated metal sheet that can be used with a profile lamp to project an image, such as leaves or prison bars
Green room	a room near to the stage where actors can relax, sometimes used to refer to the bar
Groundrow	lanterns that are fixed at floor level to light the back of the stage
Legs	curtains that mask the sides of the stage
Masking	where one actor stands directly in front of another
Practical	an item that must actually work i.e. a desk light
Prompt side	stage right – from the traditional position of the prompter
Props	short for properties – furniture, set dressing and the personal items used by the cast
Pros arch	short for proscenium – the arch at the front of the stage
Rake	the slope of the stage
Reveal	a narrow strip of wood attached to a window, or a door flat to show thickness
Revolve	a circular truck carrying two or more sets
Rig	to hang lanterns
Ros	short for rostrum, a portable raised unit to give variation in height
Set	the scenery
Set-up	when the company moves scenery and equipment into the venue
Scissors	when two actors move across each other at the same time
Slap	old fashioned term for make-up
Stage left	area of the stage to the actor's left as he faces the audience
Stage right	area of the stage to the actor's right as he faces the audience
Stage weights	heavy slabs of ironmongery, used with braces to prevent the collapse of scenery
Strike	when the company moves out of the theatre
Tabs	another word for curtains
Tech	short for technical rehearsal
Techie	affectionate term for back-stage technicians
Truck	a wheeled platform that carries scenery
Up stage	the area furthest away from the audience
Upstaging	to force an actor to speak up stage
Wings	the area to the side of the stage – unseen by audience

Tongue Twisters

Betty Botter bought a bit of butter.
'But' said she, 'this butter's bitter.
If I put it in the batter,
It will make my batter bitter.
But a bit of better butter,
That would make my batter better.'

So Betty Botter bought a bit of better butter,
Better than her bitter butter,
And she put it in her bitter batter
And made her bitter batter better.

* * * *

Red lorry, yellow lorry, red lorry, yellow lorry.

* * * *

The sixth sick sheik's sixth sheep's sick.

* * * *

I'm not the pheasant plucker, I'm the pheasant plucker's son. I'm only plucking pheasants till the pheasant plucker comes.

* * * *

The Leith police dismisseth us.

* * * *

Sister Susie's sewing shirts for sailors.

* * * *

Round the rugged rock the rugged rascal ran.

* * * *

Six packets of best mixed biscuits

* * * *

Peggy Babcock, Peggy Babcock

* * * *

Do breath tests test the breath?
Yes, that's the best of a breath test.
And the best test of the best breath
Is that the best breath stands the breath test best.

Checklists and Notes

Director's notes

Is it in the interests of the production?

Can we afford it?

If it moves, check it!

Never trust anyone – not even yourself!

It will be all right on the night – maybe?

Actors, once backstage, go deaf and blind, but rarely dumb.

Whatever can go wrong, will go wrong.

I wish we had another week.

Wouldn't this be great without the people?

Never make a crisis out of a drama.

We do this for fun – don't we?!

Rehearsal schedule

This schedule is built around a group that meets twice a week and has a ten week rehearsal period. The play is assumed to have three acts and be 80 pages in length.

No schedule ever turns out precisely as you planned it, but this should give you a starting point to create one that suits you.

Week 10

1.   Block pages 1-15
2.   Block pages 16–30 – or complete Act 1

Week 9

3.   Block the first half of Act II
4.   Finish Act II

Week 8

5.   Block the first half of Act III
6.   Finish Act III

Week 7 – Introduce working props from now on

7.   Detail work Act I
8.   Complete detail Act I

Week 6

9.   Detail work Act II
10. Complete detail work Act II

Week 5

11. Detail on Act III
12. Complete detail Act III

BOOKS   DOWN!

Week 4

13. Run whole play!
    (Sound, lights and stage management should be at this one)
14. Sticky Bits – to be confirmed

Week 3

15. To be confirmed
16. Run Act 1 x2
    (with sound effects from now on)

Week 2

17. Run Act II x2
18. Run Act III x2

Week 1

19. Run whole play
20. Run whole play

SHOW WEEK

Technical Rehearsal
Dress Rehearsal

BREAK A LEG!

Properties check list

ITEM	SOURCE	NOTES	ARRIVING	RETURNING	COST
Silver Tray	Janice		with Jan Date:	with Jan Date:	
Cocktail Glasses	group stock	15 (1 broken)	props collect from Sue	with Sue	
Magic Flowers	Magic Mart	on hire	by post Date:	post asap	£25
Sofa	to buy		on van run	to store	£50 (max)

Wardrobe notes

Measurement Chart

SHOW:

NAME: CHARACTER:

HEIGHT:

CHEST/BUST:

WAIST:

HIPS:

FRONT NAPE TO WAIST:

BACK NAPE TO WAIST:

ACROSS FRONT:

ACROSS BACK – SHOULDER TO SHOULDER:

WAIST TO KNEE:

WAIST TO ANKLE:

INSIDE ARM:

OUTSIDE LEG:

NECK/COLLAR SIZE:

HEAD:

NAPE TO GROUND:

SHOE SIZE:

GLOVE SIZE:

Wardrobe check list

CHARACTER:

ACT1

ITEM	SOURCE	NOTES	ARRIVING	RETURNING	COST
Boots	hire shop	Date: With Mike	Date: Mike	felt on heels needed	£5
Green Skirt	group stock	Date:	Date:		
Blouse	charity shop	Ruth to buy asap	to stock		£ ?
Cloak	hire	Date: Ruth	Date: Ruth	full length if possible	£15

ACT II
Repeat as before and so on.

Production check list

The following is a model to help you create a list that is adapted for your company. The list includes crucial elements in the production process that can result in major problems if neglected – I'm sure you can think of many more! It does not include details of prop and costume hire, but the production manager should keep a list similar to the heads of these departments, as printed earlier.

TITLE: SHOW DATES: d / m / y –   /   /   /

DIRECTOR:

PERFORMING RIGHTS:
Application sent: d / m / y /
License received: /   /   /

Scripts ordered: /   /   /
Received: /   /   /

Venue booked: /   /   /
Venue confirmed: /   /   /

REHEARSAL:
Dates: e.g. every Tues and Thurs from   /   /   / until   /   /   /

Venue booked: /   /   /

BACKSTAGE:

Contact list completed: ☐

Backstage meeting 1
Date:
Venue:

Backstage meeting 2
Date:
Venue:

Set design completed: ☐

Publicity notes

Poster design completed: ☐
Leaflets/posters printed: ☐
Photo call arranged: ☐
Date:
Venue:

Front of house notes

Licence applied for date:
Licence granted:
Name of licensee:

Drinks ordered: ☐
Glasses ordered: ☐
FOH team assembled: ☐

Set build/strike notes

Lighting hired: ☐
Company:
Contact No.:

Sound hired: ☐
Company:
Contact No.:

Van hire for build: Date: .....
Company:
Driver:

Van hire for strike: Date: .....
Company:
Driver:

Crew notified: ☐

Useful Contacts

Associations

GoDA
Guild of Drama Adjudicators
Hon Secretary
14 Elmwood,
Welwyn Garden City
Herts AL8 6LE
www.amdram.co.uk/goda

NDFA
National drama Festival Association
Hon Secretary
Bramleys
Main Street,
Shudy Camps
Cambridge CB1 6RA
01799 584920
www.amdram.co.uk/ndfa

NODA
National Operatic and Dramatic Association
58-60 Lincoln Road
Peterborough PE1 2RZ
0870 770 2480
www.noda.co.uk

Lighting & sound

British Library Sound Archive
96 Euston road
London NW1 2DB
020 7412 7440
www.bl.uk/catalogues/sound.html

Lancelyn Theatre Supplies
Electric Avenue
Ferry Hinksey Road
Oxford OX2 0BY
01865 722468
www.lancelyn.co.uk

Whitelight (electrics) Ltd
20 Merton Industrial Park
Jubilee Way
Wimbledon
SW19 3WL
020 8254 4800
www.Whitelight.ltd.uk

Performing rights

The Performing Right Society Ltd
29-33 Berners Street
London W1T 3AB
020 7306 5544
www.prs.co.uk

Printing

Cowdall's Printing Co.
PO Box 1,
Flag Lane,
Crewe,
Cheshire.
CW1 3BQ
01270 212389

Safety in the theatre

Health and Safety Executive

Free downloads available from the web site :
www.hse.gov.uk/pubns/entindex.htm

HSE Infoline
Caerphilly Business Park
Caerphilly
CF83 3GG
Tel: 08701 545500
e-mail: hseinformationservices@natbrit.com

Scripts

Samuel French Ltd
52 Fitzroy Street,
London W1P 6JR
020 7255 4300
www.samuelfrench-london.co.uk

Josef Weinberger Plays
12-14 Mortimer Street
London W1T 3JJ
020 7580 2827
www.josef-weinberger.com

Tricks and illusions

The Magical Mart
www.johnstylesentertainer.co.uk/mm/mm/html

Index